This book is to be returned on or before the last date below.
You may renew the book unless it is requested by another borrower.
THANK YOU FOR USING YOUR LIBRARY

OAKHAM LIBRARY
01384 255563   1 1 MAR 2011

  - 3 NOV 2004
                    1 3 FEB 2012
  1 4 SEP 2005

1 7 OCT 2005
    1 4 DEC 2005

  - 6 MAR 2006

  1 2 APR 2006
  1 0 NOV 2006

  1 4 APR 2008

    8 JAN 2010
    - 8 NOV 2010

- 6 DEC 2010
  1 0 JAN 2011
    1 4 FEB 2011

Guide for GCSE

rie Hall
her Brennand

SANDWELL LIBRARIES

I 1943092

Picture Credits

The authors and publishers would like to thank the following for permission to reproduce material in this book:

Page 4, © CORBIS; page 14, Maggie Murray/Photofusion; page 69, Ron Gregory/Life File Photo Library; page 70, Jacky Chapman/Photofusion; page 71, Michael Strang; page 72 (top and bottom), Michael Strang; page 74, Arthur Jumper/Life File Photo Library; page 78, Sally & Richard Greenhill; page 79, Heather Brennand; page 80, Sally & Richard Greenhill; page 81, Sally & Richard Greenhill; page 82, © Bryn Colton/Assignments Photographers/CORBIS; page 84, Nicola Sutton/Life File Photo Library; page 87, Michael Strang; page 92, Bubbles; page 93, Bubbles; page 94 (top), Maggie Murray/Photofusion; page 94 (bottom), Bubbles; page 95, Michael Strang; page 96, Bubbles; page 97, Bubbles; page 99, Bubbles; page 101, Bubbles; page 104 (left), Bob Battersby; page 104 (right), © O'Brien Productions/CORBIS; page 108, Mike Potter/Life File Photo Library; page 112, Bubbles; page 113, Michael Strang; page 115, Nicola Sutton/Life File Photo Library; page 117, Bubbles; page 118 (bottom), Michael Strang; page 118 (top), © CORBIS; page 119, Bubbles; page 120, Nicola Sutton/Life File Photo Library; page 126, Nicola Sutton/Life File Photo Library; page 129, Andrew Ward/Life File Photo Library; page 130, Nicola Sutton/Life File Photo Library; page 131, Bubbles; page 135, Jan Suttle/Life File Photo Library; page 136, Bubbles; page 139, Heather Brennand; page 140, Bubbles; page 141, Nicola Sutton/Life File Photo Library; page 142, Philip Woolf; page 143, Angela Maynard/Life File Photo Library; page 144, Emma Lee/Life File Photo Library; page 145, Nicola Sutton/Life File Photo Library; page 146, Bubbles; page 147, Nicola Sutton/Life File Photo Library; page 148, Mike Potter/Life File Photo Library.

Every effort has been made to obtain necessary permission with reference to copyright material. The publishers apologise if inadvertently any sources remain unacknowledged and will be glad to make the necessary arrangements at the earliest opportunity.

Orders: please contact Bookpoint Ltd, 130 Milton Park, Abingdon, Oxon OX14 4SB. Telephone: (44) 01235 827720. Fax: (44) 01235 400454. Lines are open from 9.00–6.00, Monday to Saturday, with a 24-hour message answering service. You can also order through our website www.hodderheadline.co.uk.

British Library Cataloguing in Publication Data
A catalogue record for this title is available from the British Library

ISBN 0 340 81344X

First published 2004
Impression number   10 9 8 7 6 5 4 3 2 1
Year   2007 2006 2005 2004

Copyright © 2004 Valerie Hall and Heather Brennand

All rights reserved. No part of this publication except the appendices may be reproduced or transmitted in any form or by any means, electronic or mechanical, including photocopy, recording, or any information storage and retrieval system, without permission in writing from the publisher or under licence from the Copyright Licensing Agency Limited. Further details of such licences (for reprographic reproduction) may be obtained from the Copyright Licensing Agency Limited, of 90 Tottenham Court Road, London W1T 4LP.

Typeset by Fakenham Photosetting Limited, Fakenham, Norfolk.
Printed in Italy for Hodder & Stoughton Educational, a division of Hodder Headline plc, 338 Euston Road, London NW1 3BH.

Contents

Introduction

This book has been written in response to the demand from students and teachers for a book concentrating on the coursework element of GCSE Child Development, and as a companion text to the highly successful *Child Development: A Comprehensive Text for GCSE*. Although written to support the coursework component of the AQA specification, it will be of value to students following similar GCSE, CACHE, GNVQ and other child care courses.

The book provides essential information on planning, organising, observing, recording and evaluating activities and observations of children. It is divided into six main sections as follows.

Section 1 The coursework provides an overview of the specification requirement for the coursework component and outlines the assessment criteria, explaining some of the skills and outcomes required for success.

Section 2 Step-by-step guide to the child study looks at the coursework component in more detail. It examines and explains each of the specification requirements clearly and simply, and provides a clear framework for completing the study.

Section 3 What about research? takes a closer look at a wide variety of both primary and secondary research techniques, and gives advice on planning, analysing and evaluating research.

Section 4 Broad and focused research initially identifies a range of possible ideas for wider research, which could be appropriate for the growth and development of the child being studied. This section then develops further each idea, which should lead to more specifically focused research. Further realistic suggestions for suitable activities, research and observations are included, which could form the basis of the focused area of research (FAR) investigations within the visits.

Section 5 Practical activities and investigations is a major section of the book and offers a wide range of ideas for activities/investigations on the following topics:

Creative play
Imaginative play
Food and cooking
Books and stories
Letters, words and numbers
Music and movement
Physical outdoor play
Sand and water play
Activities for babies

As well as suggesting ideas, there are tips on planning and organising coursework, and on health and safety. Additionally each type of activity includes an invaluable colour-coded section which links with Section 6, outlining how learning and development can be enhanced. As well as improving understanding this will help to select appropriate activities and identify realistic aims and expectations for the age and stage of the child.

Section 6 Development of the child   looks at the four main areas of development (physical, intellectual, emotional and social) from birth to 5 years. It is organised in a user-friendly way, is chronological and colour coded, making referencing easier, and includes ideas for games, toys and activities for each age group. It will be of great value when planning activities and visits, identifying aims and expectations when evaluating observations.

The Appendices   include a range of photocopiable materials including sample templates, e.g. writing up visits, evaluating observations, risk assessment, as well as word banks and websites.

Throughout the book there are useful tips, points to remember and ideas, clearly identified using symbols and colour coding.

ACKNOWLEDGEMENTS

The authors and publishers would like to thank Alison Oakes at AQA for her advice and support, and Stephanie Burtt who enabled us to complete the book.

We particularly wish to acknowledge Eileen Nicholson, Enid Rees and Judith Fairclough for their previous development work and continued support.

Valerie Hall:

Thanks to my family: Ken, Samantha and Darren, for their patience and support.

Heather Brennand:

I would like to thank my husband, Dave, and children, James and Rachel, for their patience and understanding, and a special thanks to mum and dad for their continued encouragement.

The coursework

In this section we will look at what is involved in the child study for your GCSE examination.

 ## GCSE CHILD DEVELOPMENT COURSEWORK

WHAT'S IT ALL ABOUT?

The child development examination for most GCSE Home Economics: Child Development courses consists of:

1. a written paper;

2. a piece of coursework.

The written paper tests your knowledge and understanding of all of the different aspects and areas of the course under exam conditions. The coursework is usually in the form of a child study or an observation study. This is where you have the chance to show your understanding of how a child learns and develops, by studying and working with a child over a set period of time.

This is often worth 50 per cent of the final mark.

WHAT SHOULD BE INCLUDED IN A CHILD STUDY?

This will depend on which examination board you are using, and your teachers will help you with this.

The following is an outline of the child study for the AQA examination board.

Child study outline from the AQA examination board

Introduction

This is a section describing the child at the beginning of the study period.

You should include things like a description of what the child looks like, as well as information about family, the local environment and stages of physical, emotional and social development.

Broad area of research

At the end of your introduction, you should choose an area from the course to research. This should be something you are interested in, but should also be an area that you think is important for your child's development.

You should now research this area. This will probably be mostly secondary research.

You need to analyse and evaluate what you have found out.

Focused area of research

From your general background research, you need to choose a more specific area to research further, and to investigate during your visits.

For this you should try to include both primary and secondary research.

You should evaluate this research and use it to plan activities and/or investigations for your visits.

Visiting and observing the child

You need to carry out six visits to your child spread over six months.

During these visits you need to plan suitable, interesting activities that will help you to see how your child reacts, grows, changes and develops.

In at least three of your visits you need to plan activities or investigations linked to your focused area of research.

Your visits should be evaluated.

Final evaluation

This is the last section of the study.

You should look back over all your work and try to identify what you have learnt about *both* the child you are studying *and* your chosen area of research.

Bibliography

A list of all the books, leaflets and websites you have used.

 MANAGING THE CHILD STUDY

Just like any other piece of work, your child study needs to be planned and organised. That way you will:

- know what you need to do;
- know when it needs to be done by;
- earn good marks;
- not get too stressed!

When marking your child study, *among other things* your teacher will be looking for:

- research;
- evidence of planning and organisation;
- evaluation;
- personal opinions;
- quotes and use of specialist words;
- presentation.

MORE ABOUT RESEARCH

> **Keywords**
>
> **To research:**
> 'to carry out investigations into a subject'
> **Investigation:**
> 'a careful search to discover facts'. (Adapted from *Collins Concise Dictionary*)

Although your coursework is called a 'child study' it is really a research study, because you are being asked to use research (information gathered) and then use it to show that you understand how and why children learn and develop.

There are three areas of research required for a child study.

1. **Researching development** – how children develop and change physically, intellectually, emotionally and socially, and how we can help them to do this.

2. **Broad research** – this is the research you do on a broad topic you are interested in, but also one which you think is important for your child's learning and development, e.g. play, intellectual development and toys.

3. **Focused research** – this should be a topic taken from your broad area of research that you should investigate in more detail.
   For example, from a broad area of research into **play**, you might decide to focus on creative play or safety of play. Alternatively, from a broad area of research into **intellectual development** you might decide to focus on concepts.

What have you learnt from all three types of research should then be used to plan and carry out visits, activities and investigations for your child study.

Young boy flying a kite enjoying outdoor play

➡ MORE ABOUT PLANNING AND ORGANISING

It is very important to plan and organise your study. Your teacher will give you lots of help to organise your study and to break it down into 'bite-sized pieces'. You will be given lots of activities to help you to understand the coursework and to improve your skills.

You will probably be given targets or deadlines for handing in different sections of the study. Your work will also be checked regularly by your teacher and you will be given feedback that will give you ideas and targets to help you improve.

TOP TIPS	

- If you do not understand, ask the teacher.
- Do not leave everything until the last minute.
- Find out what the deadlines are for each piece of work.
- Know when the final deadline is for the completed study to be handed in.
- Put all your dates into a planner or diary.
- Use a checklist to help you to organise the study (see Appendix 2).
- Keep your notes in a safe place.
- Use separate wallets or folders to keep each section of the study separate – then your work will not be muddled.
- Put a label or colour code on the front of each wallet or folder so you know easily what is in it.
- Try to show evidence of your planning in your study, e.g.
  - a plan showing what you will research, where you will get information, how you will present it.
  - a chart showing the planning of activities and investigations for your visits (see Appendix 5 for an example).
- Plan your visits over a reasonable amount of time so that you are more likely to see changes in your child's development.
- Act upon any feedback from your teacher.

MORE ABOUT EVALUATION

You need to **evaluate** throughout your study. This means looking at different stages of your study and picking out *what* you think you have learnt that it is important and *why* it is important.

MORE ABOUT PERSONAL OPINIONS

Personal opinions are your own thoughts, ideas and views about the child you are studying. As you get to know the child you are studying and learn more about development you may feel more confident to give your own views and ideas.

To gain higher marks try to find quotes or references to back up your opinions.

Remember:

You are not an expert in Child Development so take care with what personal opinions you give. You do not want to upset the family.

 MORE ABOUT QUOTES AND SPECIALIST TERMS

At various points in your study, you need to try and use specialist terms and quotes to show that you really know and understand what you are talking about. This is especially important for:

- the introduction;
- the planning and writing up of visits;
- the evaluation; and
- wherever you have given personal opinion.

SPECIALIST TERMS

It is better to say,
> *'he picked up the pencil using a mature pincer grasp and began to colour in the picture;'*

than to say,
> *'he picked up the pencil and coloured in.'*

QUOTES

These are short statements copied from textbooks. They must be written within inverted commas (speech marks).

If you use short statements copied from textbooks, you need to say in some way where you have taken them from. For example,

'According to Brennand *et al.* a child of two *"uses a mature pincer grasp to pick up and place small objects"*.'

➡ MORE ABOUT PRESENTATION

You will probably find out a lot of information during your research. At this stage you will have to select which information is really useful.

Once you have decided which information you want to include there are many ways to present it. The diagram on the next page will give you some ideas.

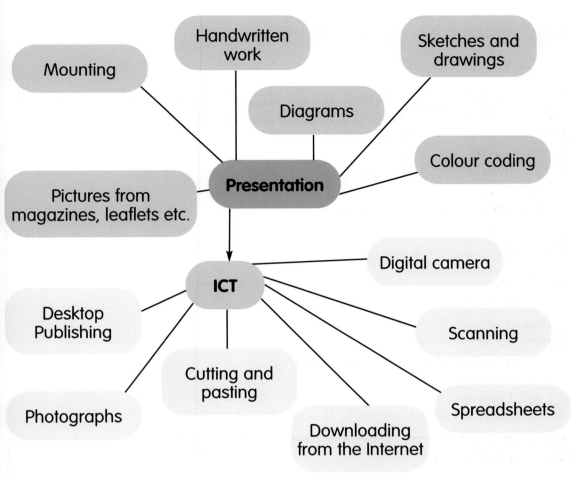

All these aspects work together (inter-relate) to complete the final picture.

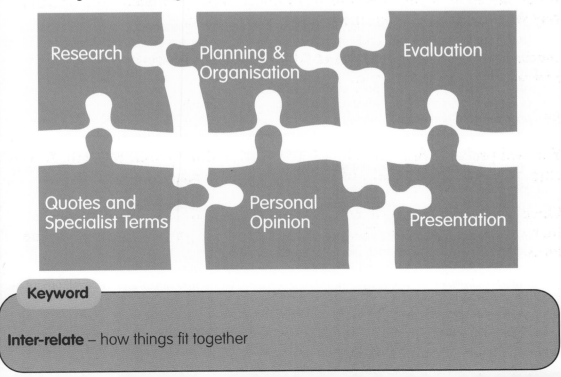

Keyword

Inter-relate – how things fit together

➡️ WHAT ABOUT ASSESSMENT

The child study is marked out of 105.

The mark is divided into the following six areas:

Knowledge and understanding	20
Identifying issues, hypotheses, expectations	20
Selection and use of skills	20
Gather, record and collate information from a variety of sources	25
Evaluation of the study	15
Quality of written communication	5
Total	**105**

These headings are for teachers to use.

To help you understand how your study will be marked, the following table shows some of the things teachers will be looking for.

Knowledge and understanding   **20 marks**

To gain good marks you will need to have:
- shown knowledge and understanding of all areas of physical, intellectual, emotional and social development;
- shown knowledge and understanding of your chosen area of research;
- used your knowledge and understanding to plan and organise research, activities and investigations for research and visits, aims and expectations, and observations and evaluations;
- used specialist terms in all parts of your study;
- given **your** opinions about what you have seen and found out;
- used relevant quotes and references.

Identifying issues, hypotheses, expectations   **20 marks**

To gain good marks you will need to have:
- chosen an area to research that is important to your child's development;
- used both primary and secondary resources;
- used different methods of research;
- explained why you think each piece of research is important.

In planning your observations and FAR activities, you need to have:
- chosen activities and investigations that are suitable for the age and stage of development of the child;
- given clear aims for visits and investigations;
- given clear expectations/predictions of what you expect to find out.

Selection and use of skills   20 marks

To gain good marks you will need to have:
- used a good range of skills, e.g.
    questionnaires;
    interviews;
    use of the Internet;
    textbooks;
    ICT;
    activities for visits.

Gather, record and collate information from a variety of sources   25 marks

To gain good marks you will need to have:
- completed all parts of your study;
- used clear headings for each part of your study;
- used different methods of presentation;
- selected appropriate and useful information from your research.
You also need to make sure that:
- your work is well organised and presented;
- your work is easy to read.

Evaluation   15 marks

To gain good marks you will need to have:
- evaluated each piece of research you did;
- evaluated each visit;
- evaluated each FAR activity or investigation;
- completed a final evaluation of your study;
- used specialist terms, quotes and references;
- given personal opinions.

Quality of written communication   5 marks

To gain good marks you will need to have:
- good spelling, punctuation and grammar;
- clear, organised and well presented work.

2 Step-by-step guide to the child study

In this section we will look in more detail at what needs to be included in your child study. You will be given ideas, examples, tips and techniques that will help you to plan and organise your work. You don't have to use them all.

➡ CHOOSING A CHILD TO STUDY

The first thing you need to do is to choose a child to study! You will need to ask the parent's permission because you will need to have regular contact with them, the child and possibly other members of the family over quite a long period of time.

!

Remember:

The exam board states that you must study:

■ *'a single child between 0–5 years'.*

- ✏ If possible, try to avoid studying a new, or very young baby. Young babies tend to spend a lot of time sleeping!
- ✏ Choosing an older child can be difficult. By the age of 5 their development is beginning to slow down and even out, so you may not see as much change and progression.
- ✏ Try not to study a twin – it's difficult to work with one and ignore the other one.
- ✏ Studying younger brothers and sisters may also be a problem. Because you probably see them so often it is not always easy to note changes and progression.

Remember:

The aim of the course is to study about **average** learning and development. Choosing a child with a disability may make this difficult to do.

Whoever you choose to study, you must make sure that no one will be able to recognise or identify the child or family. You can use the child's first name, as well as other family first names, but . . .
do *not* include:

◆ surnames;
◆ addresses or telephone numbers;
◆ street names or house numbers;
◆ maps showing area and/or child's home;
◆ copies of letters with names/addresses.

Once you have the parents' permission you are ready to start your study with the following.

➡ STEP 1 – THE INTRODUCTION

This should be a fairly detailed description of the child. It should include what the child looks like and can do at the beginning of the study so that the person reading it has a clear picture of the child.

Don't expect to be able to get all the information you need at one visit – you might have to make two or three short visits close together. You might also need to ask the parents questions about something that you have not been able to see the child do, but try to rely more on your own observations.

Remember:

Don't give detailed background information about where and when born, weight at birth, first tooth, first steps, first word and so on *unless you are studying a new baby* – it won't get you extra marks.

You should include all of the following

A PHYSICAL DESCRIPTION

You need to give the date of birth and the age of child at the start of the study – in years and months or months and weeks. Think about what the child looks like. You could include information on:
- height and weight;
- shape of face, nose and mouth;
- hair colour and style;
- eye colour and shape;
- freckles and dimples;
- build – slim, plump, sturdy;
- number of teeth – which ones;
- complexion/skin colour;
- hands and feet.

Think about whether the child is an 'average' size for their age – refer to textbooks to support your opinion.

PERSONALITY

Try to describe the child's personality. For example is the child:
- happy;
- loving;
- outgoing;
- extrovert;
- mischievous;
- quiet;
- shy;
- timid;
- lively;
- afraid;
- easily bored;
- temperamental?

Try to describe how the child shows their personality.

FAMILY BACKGROUND

Include any relevant information about the child's family. For example is the child:
- an only child;
- a youngest, oldest, middle child etc.;
- an only boy/girl?

Try to explain how you think this might affect the child's development and behaviour, or the way the parents treat it.

What about the family group? Is it:
- nuclear;
- one parent;
- adopted;
- step;
- part of a large family;
- extended family?

Do parent/s work? Who looks after the child if or when parents are not there? Do the family spend time together – when – where?

Again try to explain how you think this might affect the child.

HOME AND LOCAL AREA

Briefly describe the child's home. Think about the following:
- Do they have their own bedroom or share;
- Is there an area both inside and outside to play;
- Are there any safety precautions;
- Do they have lots of toys and books? What sort?

Then briefly describe the local area.
- What type of area is it – small village;
  – town;
  – city suburb?
- What about playgroups, mother and toddler groups, nurseries?

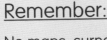 Remember:

No maps, surnames, addresses, etc.

PHYSICAL DEVELOPMENT

Study the child's **gross motor skills**.

Can they:
- crawl;
- walk;
- climb;
- hop;
- skip;
- jump;
- balance;
- climb stairs;
- throw a ball;
- catch a ball;
- kick a ball;
- ride a tricycle?

Toddler showing gross motor skills climbing stairs

Don't just list the skills. Try to describe *how* they do them.

Then look at **fine motor skills**.

Can the child:
- pick up small things;
- place things down carefully;
- hold things;
- turn knobs;
- fasten buttons and zips;
- build with bricks;
- hold a pen, pencil or crayon;
- draw;
- thread beads;
- do jigsaws etc.?

Again, describe **how** they do these things. Try to include **specialist terms**, e.g. *pincer grasp, tripod grasp*.

SENSORY DEVELOPMENT

How does the child use its **senses** to explore:

- sight;
- touch;
- hearing;
- taste;
- smell.

Young children explore everything with their mouths (**mouthing**) but all children need to have a chance to explore, touch and feel different materials. What toys or activities does the child have which would help them to do this?

INTELLECTUAL DEVELOPMENT
Language skills

- Look at how well can they talk and communicate.
- Do they use sounds, single words, short phrases or complete sentences? Try to give examples.
- Do they use hands to help them communicate, e.g. pointing?
- Can they understand more than they can use? Give examples.
- What sort of words do they know – family names, household objects, toys, etc.?
- How do the parents encourage language development?
- Do they know simple songs or nursery rhymes? Which ones?
- Do they have speech difficulties? Give examples.
- If you write down words or phrases the child is using now, at the end of your study you will be able to compare how they talk with the start of the study. This way you will be able to highlight how they have improved.

Cognitive development

Describe what the child knows and understands.

Do they understand anything about:

- colour;
- size;
- numbers;
- letters;
- time;
- past, present, future;
- big/little;
- cause and effect;
- object permanence;
- shape;
- floating/sinking?

Again, try to give examples.

SOCIAL DEVELOPMENT

This is how the child behaves, acts and plays. Think about whether the child:

- is usually well behaved;
- says please and thank you;
- shares things;
- takes turns when playing;
- behaves differently with
  - family
  - strangers
  - other children;
- gets on well with adults and children of all ages;
- has temper tantrums – when?
- gets plenty of chances to meet other adults and children, e.g. at playgroup, nursery, park;
- has any special friends;
- is toilet trained;
- can feed itself, wash and dry hands and face, clean teeth, get dressed.

➡ STEP 2 – BROAD AREA OF RESEARCH (BAR)

Once you have finished the introduction, you should have a good idea of what the child is like, what they can and cannot do and what they are interested in. You should now be able to choose a topic to look at in more detail, which will become your **broad area of research**.

This should be:

- based on what you know about the child's age, interests and stage of development;
- an area you are interested in;
- a topic you think is important because it could affect your child's learning and development in some way;
- something you can research easily.

Remember:

You need to show how your broad area of research links with the child you are studying. Give reasons for what you have chosen and why. For example:

'From my introductory visit, I know that Rachael enjoys all sorts of play,

but probably likes to be outside more than inside. She is very energetic and her gross motor skills are good, so she enjoys running around, riding her tricycle and playing with a football.

She is also quite creative and imaginative, and enjoys making things and building with lego. However, she does get frustrated easily if she cannot do something right.

Rachael has lots of friends, both close to where she lives and at nursery. She loves to dress up and play pretend games with them.

From my observations Rachael is obviously interested in all types of play, and play is important for her.

So I have decided to choose "play" as my broad area of research.'

Now you are ready to **research** your chosen area. This should be **background research** – general information which will help *you* understand more about the area you have chosen (see Section 4).

At this stage most of your research will probably come from **secondary sources** (see page 25).

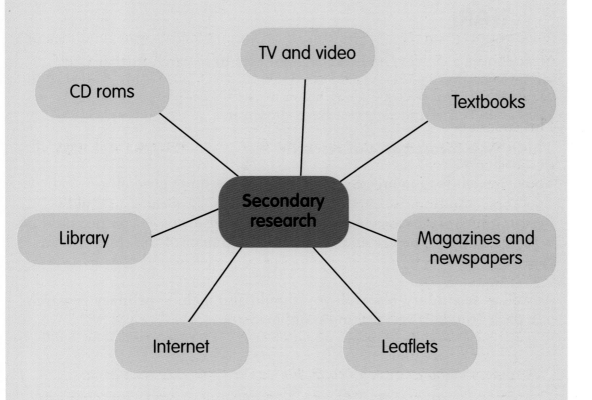

Remember:

State where you got your information. This will show how much work and reading you have done

Don't do so much research for your broad area that you have nothing left to find out for your focused research!

Evaluation of research

Look at what you have found out. How useful is it? What have you learnt? *Write a short summary.*

Link your research to what you know about your child and what you wrote at the end of the introduction.

 # STEP 3 – FOCUSED AREA OF RESEARCH (FAR)

Next choose a *smaller, more manageable* area to research further (see section 4).

State *what* this is and *why* you have chosen it.

This is your **focused area of research**.

Your research for the broad area will have been quite general.

Research for your focused area needs to be *more detailed*. You need to link it more closely to the age and stage of development of the child you are studying.

As well as **secondary research** you should also include **primary research** (see page 26). This will get you more marks.

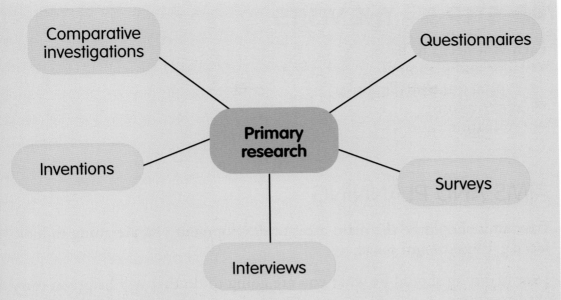

Evaluation of focused area of research

- Briefly evaluate each piece of research you have done, and say how useful each is.
- Decide how you can use your focused area of research in your visits. State this clearly.
- Predict what you expect to find out.
- Plan your visits.

STEP 4 – PLANNING THE VISITS AND FAR ACTIVITIES

You need to plan and carry out six visits over a period of six months.

For these visits try to organise activities which will help you to look at your child's physical, intellectual, emotional and social development.

In three of your visits, you also need to do an activity or investigation linked to your focused area of research.

Include a simple plan for your visits. This will earn you marks for planning.

For an example see Appendix 5.

STEP 5 – THE VISITS

Each visit needs to have:
- aims and planning;
- expectations/predictions;
- observations;
- evaluation.

AIMS AND PLANNING

Your aims should be the main areas of development you are going to look for, e.g. physical and social.

Your planning should be what you are going to do that will help you carry out these aims.

You need to write these down clearly in your own words. Try not to be too vague!

It is much better to say,

> *'my aim for the visit is to look at James' physical development especially his fine and gross motor skills by weighing, measuring, mixing, shaping and decorating small cakes';*

than to say,

> *'I am going to look at James' physical skills by cooking.'*

When planning, try to think about all of the following:
- where you will carry out the visit;
- what you will need;
- safety;
- if the activity is suitable for the age of the child;
- if the activity will let you achieve your aims.

EXPECTATIONS/PREDICTIONS

These are what you think will happen for each of the main areas of development you are looking at.
- You need to give reasons *why* you think they will happen.
- You should try to link this to what you know about average development for the age of your child.
- Try to give references from appropriate textbooks.

For example,

> 'Socially I expect that he will be able to play happily alongside Steven because according to Brennand *et al* a child of two should *"begin to enjoy parallel play"*.'

Try to give several expectations for each of the areas of development you are looking at.

OBSERVATIONS

TOP TIPS

- In your observations you should describe exactly what happened during the visit.
- The visit should start when you arrive and finish when you leave.

Don't just write about the activities you planned and how they worked. If you do this, you could miss a lot of other interesting details, which might help other areas of development.

Give as much detail as possible.

EVALUATION

At the end of each visit you need to analyse and evaluate what you have found out.

TOP TIPS

- Look firstly at the areas of development you said you would look at in your aims.
- What did you expect to find?
- What did you actually find?
- Were there any differences between what you expected to see and what actually did see?
- Try to link your ideas, opinions and observations with references to text books and average milestones.
- Don't just look at the areas of development you stated in your aims. Try to look at others as well.
- Don't be worried if your visit and/or activities were not successful. Try to explain why they were not; e.g. did you try to do something too difficult with the child? Was the child feeling unwell or upset?

FAR INVESTIGATIONS/ACTIVITIES

Your FAR investigations/activities will also need to have:

- aims;
- expectations/predictions;
- a written record;
- an evaluation.

However, your FAR investigations and activities may not be as long or detailed as the rest of the visit. It will depend on whether you are doing an investigation or an activity (see section 4).

TOP TIP

Your FAR investigation or activity could be written up as part of the whole visit or separately. See Appendix 3.

 STEP 6 – FINAL EVALUATION

This is the last section of your study.

You need to use this final evaluation to:

- show how your child has changed and developed;
- look at how successful your research has been.

TOP TIPS

- Begin by reading through your introduction.
- Use the same headings as in your introduction so that you can identify how the child has changed and developed.
- Try to make references to exact visits or activities where you realised the child had learnt something new or how to do something better.
- Include quotes and references.
- Use specialist terms where you can, e.g. pincer grasp, egocentric, solitary play.
- Give your own opinions but give reasons as well.
- Say what you have learnt from your research, FAR investigations and activities, and observations.

STEP 7 – BIBLIOGRAPHY

Finally, list all the books, magazines, websites, computer software, etc. you have used.

 ## STEP 8 – APPENDIX

Include any research materials, e.g. leaflets, examples of child's work, that you have used.

3 What about research?

Research is one of the most important parts of your child study. There are two different types of research:

- **SECONDARY RESEARCH** – this is research which may help you, but which other people have already done, e.g. information from a text book;
- **PRIMARY RESEARCH** – this is your own information which you have got yourself, e.g. from questionnaires.

One of the main sources for your child study will be your own observation of the child.

! Remember:

Remember that research is not just copying huge chunks of information from a textbook or printing off lots of information from a website. You need to:

- ◆ select (pick out) what you think is important and useful;
- ◆ present it in an interesting and varied way;
- ◆ try to put it in your own words;
- ◆ evaluate (say what you have learnt from it that is important and will help you in some way).

BOOKS AND MAGAZINES

The textbooks from your child development area will give you a lot of information but don't forget, books from other areas might help as well.

Try your school and local library. Ask the librarian and they will help you search for information.

TV PROGRAMMES AND VIDEOS

You may be able to borrow videos from school or from your local clinic/health centre.

Look out for useful programmes on TV – even children's programmes such as 'The Tweenies' could help you if you are looking at how children learn.

Secondary research

INTERNET

You can find a lot of information on lots of subjects, but it can take up a lot of time and not all of it will be relevant!

You will need to spend time sorting it and picking out what is really useful. Don't just print off everything you find.

NEWSPAPERS

You can often find useful articles and news reports that might help your research. If your family don't buy a paper you will find newspapers in libraries. You can often find back copies there as well.

LEAFLETS, BOOKLETS ETC.

You can get these from supermarkets, health centres and clinics, chemists, dentists etc. They are usually free and will give you:

- lots of information;
- ideas for presentations;
- useful illustrations.

QUESTIONNAIRES AND SURVEYS

This can provide you with a lot of useful information *if* you design it carefully.

- Think carefully about what you need to know.
- Make sure your questions are clear and simple.
- Try to use mainly closed questions – ones that people can answer with a tick or cross.
- Make sure you choose your target group carefully.
- Try to ask 15–20 people to get good results.
- Check your questionnaire with your teacher first.

VISITS

Visits to toy shops, nurseries, play areas, museums etc. can give you lots of useful information.

ASK 'EXPERTS'

Parents, grandparents, cousins, siblings and friends are all experts! They give you lots of ideas and information.

COMPARATIVE INVESTIGATION

You could carry out a comparative investigation in a shop, nursery etc., e.g.

- compare play activities at home with a nursery;
- compare how different toys might encourage different areas of development;
- compare prices of similar products in different shops

Primary research

PERSONAL EXPERIENCES

Think about what you already know – what you know and have learnt.

PHOTOGRAPHS

Take a camera with you when you are doing research, e.g. on your child study observations, to a nursery school (you may need permission). You can use the photos as evidence and comment on them.

LETTERS AND EMAIL

You can write to relevant manufactures and other companies and organisations such as ROSPA, or to 'experts', e.g. health visitor.

- You need to write the letters carefully. Make it very clear *what* information you need and *why*.
- You may have a better chance of a reply if you include a stamped, addressed envelope.

However, remember that companies get hundreds of requests every day – so you may not get any reply.

INTERVIEW

This can be used to find out people's ideas, opinions and experiences. You can do this:

- face to face;
- by telephone;
- group discussion;
- video-conferencing.

Choose who to interview carefully and plan your questions before you go. Think about how you will record your interview – you could use a video camera or tape recorder.

➡ USING THE INTERNET

Many companies, organisations and even individual people put websites on the internet. These can provide you with lots of information that *might* be useful for your child study coursework.

Even if you don't have access to the Internet at home, you will find computers in school and libraries. Your school may also have an Intranet service. Here your child development teacher might have already listed useful websites, which could save you a lot of time.

ACCESSING INFORMATION

Finding information on the Internet is easy. Finding *relevant* information is a little more difficult. For relevant website addresses see Appendix 4.

The two main ways of accessing information are as follows.

1. Using the **website address**.
   You can find these from:
   - ➬ magazines such as *Parent, Mother and Baby*;
   - ➬ labels on toys, clothing, food, equipment;
   - ➬ through TV channels, e.g. www.bbc.co.uk

2. Using a **search engine**, such as www.ask.co.uk or www.google.co.uk. You enter a keyword or words and the search engine quickly searches websites and pages for information linked to the keywords, then lists them for you. However, if you typed in '*babies*' you are likely to get a huge list, which would take you forever to look through!
   So try to be as precise as possible. For example type in '*social play for babies*'.

!

Remember:

Finding lots of information is easy, but it's *how you use it* that is important. Don't just print off everything you see on the screen. Putting this into your coursework as research will not get you good marks!

- ◆ Take notes choosing only what is relevant – then write it up.
- ◆ Use a highlighter pen on printouts to show which bits are relevant – then comment on them.
- ◆ Cut and paste relevant sections into a Word document, then summarise and evaluate them showing what you have learnt.

USING SURVEYS AND QUESTIONNAIRES

A survey is a way of getting information. The most popular way of doing this is by a questionnaire.

WHAT IS A QUESTIONNAIRE?

A questionnaire is a set of written questions given to a number of different people to collect information.

Questionnaires can be useful to help you to find out information for your FAR. They need to be carefully planned.

TOP TIPS

Tips on **planning** questionnaires.
- Firstly, make a list of exactly what you want to find out.
- Decide whom you will ask. Only ask people who can give you the information you need.
- How many people will you ask? A minimum of 20 will make your results more worthwhile.
- Remember if you are asking 20 people you will need 20 copies of your questionnaire.

Tips on **designing** questionnaires.
- Give your questionnaire a title.
- Include a brief introduction to explain clearly who you are and why you are doing the questionnaire.
- Ask simple, clear questions that are relevant. Too many questions may confuse you when you come to analyse the answers.
- Get your teacher to check your questionnaire before you hand it out.

TYPES OF QUESTIONS

There are two types of questions – closed and open.

Closed questions limit the possible answers. They are easier to analyse than open questions and can be used to produce good graphs, charts etc. Examples of closed questions include:

1. Does your child go to nursery?

   Yes ☐

   No ☐

2. How often do you take your child to the park?

   Every day ☐

   Once a week ☐

   Once a month ☐

   Very rarely ☐

   Never ☐

3. How important do you think it is that your child mixes with other children?

   Very important ☐

   Quite important ☐

   Not very important ☐

   Not important at all ☐

4. From the following list of toys tick <u>3</u> that your child plays with most regularly.

Jigsaw	☐	Soft toys	☐
Lego	☐	Board games	☐
Doll	☐	Books	☐
Tricycle	☐	Pretend toys	☐
Play dough	☐	Dressing up	☐
Shops	☐	Paints/crayons	☐
Balls	☐	Small world	☐

Open questions ask people about their thoughts and opinions. They are more difficult to analyse than open questions because 20 different people may give 20 different answers. However, they can give more exciting results. An example of an open question is:

Why do you think it is important to spend time reading with your child?

_____

_____

_____

_____

TOP TIPS

Tips on **analysing** questionnaires.

- Collect together the results from all your questionnaires.
- Analyse each question separately.
- Present the results in a clear, colourful way using a *variety* of graphs, pie charts, bar charts, pictograms etc.
- You can do this by hand or by using a software package such as Excel.

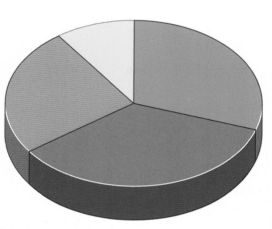

A pie chart

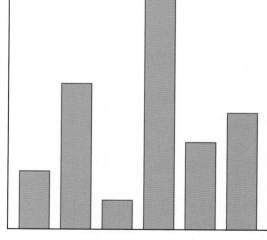

A bar graph

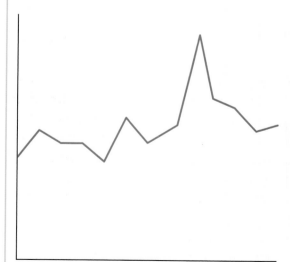

A line graph

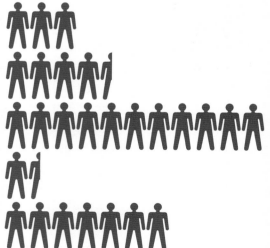

A pictograph

Finally
◆ Look back at why you carried out the questionnaire.
◆ Are your results useful?
◆ What are your conclusions?
◆ How will you use this information in the rest of your study?

Remember:

The information you find out should be linked with FAR visits.

 USING AN INTERVIEW

An interview is one-to-one primary research.

You might want to interview parents, a nursery nurse or midwife, health visitors, teachers, etc. for specialist information.

Like all other good primary research, it needs to be planned carefully and in a similar way to a questionnaire.

TOP TIPS

Tips on planning interviews.
• Firstly think about exactly what information you want to find out before you decide on the questions.
• If you are interviewing more than one person about the same topic, you need to use more structured questions (e.g. closed questions, see pages 28 and 29) so that you can compare and evaluate their answers.
• If you are only going to interview one person, you can use more open-ended questions (see page 29). This lets the person being interviewed talk more freely. Also, if they say something that you didn't expect or think about, you can ask them more about it. This way you might get more useful information.
• Think about how you are going to carry out the interview – you need a quiet, comfortable place where you will not be interrupted.
• Plan how you will record your interview. If you try to write down everything that is said, you may miss important points and will not be able to concentrate on the answer.
• Remember to write up (transcribe) the interview and then evaluate it. Pick out what you have learnt that helps you with your research.

Interview with playgroup leader

1. Do you think it is important to read books with children under 3 years of age? Why/Why not?
2. What do you understand by the term 'intellectual development'?
3. What activities do you think help intellectual development the most? Why?
4. How do you try to encourage the intellectual development of the children that come to your playgroup?
5. Do you think it is best for a child to read on his own, with an adult or in a group with children of a similar age? Why?

 ## Remember:

Once you have collected and recorded your information, analyse and evaluate your results. What have you learnt? What conclusion can you give?

 # USING AN INVENTORY

An inventory is basically a list of objects, such as:
- toys,
- games,
- books,
- safety equipment.

However, you can develop and use an inventory to make it into an easy way of collecting information so that you can **compare** and **analyse** a range of ideas.

 Think About

You will need to think about:
- What you want to find out.
- How you will collect and record your information.

The easiest way to collect and record your information is to use a **chart**. An example appears below.

Example

Inventory of the toys in a child's toybox to see how they encourage physical, intellectual, emotional and social development

Type of toy	Suitable age	P	I	E	S	Any other information
Duplo	18 + months	☺☺☺	☺	☺☺		Easy to wash Doesn't break easily Bright colour
Soft toys						
10-piece jigsaw						

Key	
☺	Encourages little development
☺☺	Encourages some development
☺☺☺	Encourages a lot of development

➡ USING COMPARATIVE INVESTIGATION

A comparative investigation can be used if you want to compare similar things to try to identify similarities and differences.

For example, if you wanted to compare different books for the age of the child you are studying, you might want to compare:
- costs;
- picture on cover;
- number of pages;
- colourful pictures;
- size of book;
- ease of turning pages;
- what it is about.

Again you need a chart so that it is easy to record your information. An example appears below.

	The Jolly Postman	Tweenies Annual	Etc.	Etc.
Cost	£7.99	£4.99		
Number of pages	10	50		
Colourful pictures	Lots of small, detailed pictures	Some very colourful, little detail		
Size of book	A5 size	A4 size – unmanagable		
Ease of turning pages	Easy – thick pages	Thin, easy to tear		
What it is about	One long story	Lots of different stories and activities		
Picture on cover	Imaginative	Bold colours – unimaginative		
Overall appeal	Good – things to do as story goes along	Good – links with TV		
Overall rating	★★★	★		

★	Poor
★★	Good
★★★	Excellent

Remember:

Again remember to evaluate and draw conclusions. Make sure you relate this to your child and/or research area.

 USING A RISK ASSESSMENT

A risk assessment is used to:
- think of (identify) any possible dangers or hazards;
- decide whether these are high, medium or low risk;
- decide what steps you would take to prevent them.

It is used in industry, hospitals and schools, but could also be used in your child study when:
- looking at safety issues – e.g. safety of toys, the home;
- planning visits, e.g. trips to the park, beach, swimming baths;
- organising practical activities, e.g. junk modelling, cooking.

You need to plan a simple form to carry out a risk assessment. An example can be seen in Appendix 6.

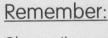 OBSERVATIONAL SKILLS

WHY DO WE OBSERVE CHILDREN?

Observing, watching and recording children's behaviour can tell us a lot about how they are **learning** and **developing**.

> **!**
>
> Remember:
>
> Observations are an example of **primary research**.

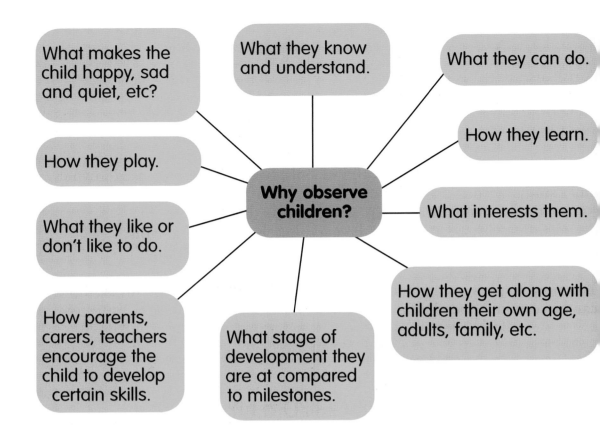

What makes the child happy, sad and quiet, etc?

What they know and understand.

What they can do.

How they play.

How they learn.

What they like or don't like to do.

Why observe children?

What interests them.

How parents, carers, teachers encourage the child to develop certain skills.

What stage of development they are at compared to milestones.

How they get along with children their own age, adults, family, etc.

OBSERVING YOUR CHILD

It can be difficult to play with your child and write down what you see at the same time.

There will be times when you may want to stand back and watch the child's involvement in the activity without doing it for them.

You will need to plan how to record your information.

TOP TIPS

Ten tips to survive your observation

1. Think about the age of the child. Don't make activities too long for a younger child, they easily become bored.
2. Children do not perform to order. Always have a couple of extra ideas just in case the child is unwilling to join in the activity you have planned.
3. Try to involve the parents and encourage their support.
4. Think about the areas of development you want to look at and then plan activities which will help to show the development.
5. Be organised and well planned. This will save time and you will get the best results.
6. Plan observation charts for specific areas of development. This will make you very focused.
7. Have a notepad and pen to record the information. The child you are studying may wish to help with this.
8. You may be able to use a Dictaphone, tape recorder, video or digital camera to help record what you have seen.
9. Don't ignore examples of behaviour/development that you did not plan to see through your activity or investigation. Children often do and say things when you least expect them to.
10. Don't forget to praise your child. You will gain a better relationship and a more willing child.

Remember:

- Visit your child regularly.
- Make sure you have six visits, which include a variety of activities.
- Try to allow the child to be as natural as possible.

WRITING UP YOUR OBSERVATIONS

The observations you make will be in the form of a written record.

- ✏ Using subheadings will help to organise your work (see Appendix 3).
- ✏ Try to describe the actual activities you have seen. Include enough detail to give the reader a clear picture of the visit.
- ✏ Tick charts can be useful to record information. The information gathered must then be written up to summarise your findings.
- ✏ When describing activities try to link what you have seen with the development of the child.

- Try to provide evidence of your activities, e.g. drawing, painting.
- You could use a digital camera to photograph stages of activities and the final product.
- Any photographic evidence, materials, results of research must be commented on to explain why they are important to the study and the child's progress.

> **!** Remember:
>
> Confidentiality is very important when using photographic evidence of the child. Take care not to expose the child's identity.
>
> **■** Be sensitive when making comments about the role of the parents and the background of the child.

 EVALUATING THE OBSERVATIONS

Your teacher may be able to show you how to evaluate your observations with a practice exercise like the one below (also see Appendix 7).

EVALUATING

Physical Development	Intellectual Development
Social Development	**Emotional Development**

- Look through your written observations.
- Try to pick out any examples of different areas of development. You have recorded from your notes.
- Put this information onto the chart.
- Look in textbooks and find at least one quote to support each box. Don't forget to state the source of information.
- Now look back at your expectations. What did you set out to achieve? Take each expectation and comment on whether or not your expectation was achieved. Try to explain why.
- Try to make the link between expectations and milestones.
- Try to link your evaluations with your expectations.
- Now write up your evaluation in more detail using these headings.

Broad and focused research

This section of the book will identify some possible **broad areas of research** to study and then give examples of how they could be developed further for the **focused area of research**.

The ideas in this section are to help you think about:

- ✏ possible broad areas of research;
- ✏ what research you could include in your broad area;
- ✏ how this could be developed for your focused area;
- ✏ some activities and investigations you might use in your visits.

Keywords

Broad area of research (BAR)
This is the topic you choose to look at after your introduction. The information should not be too detailed. It will usually come from secondary sources.

Focused area of research (FAR)
This is a smaller, more manageable area that you choose to research further. It will be more detailed and include both primary and secondary sources of information.

! Remember:

The ideas here are only suggestions. You may have other ideas which you should discuss with your teacher.

➡ BROAD AREA OF RESEARCH

Once you have finished the introduction to your study, you should have a good idea of what the child is like, what they can and cannot do and what they are interested in. You should then be able to choose a topic to look at in more detail, which will become your **broad area of research** (BAR).

This should be:

- based on what you know about the child's age, interests and stage of development;
- an area you are interested in;
- a topic you think is important because it could affect your child's learning and development in some way;
- something you can easily research;
- supported by and involve the child's parents.

SUGGESTIONS FOR BROAD AREAS OF RESEARCH (BAR)

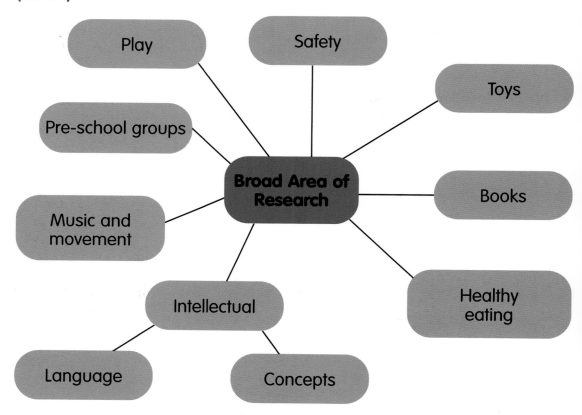

TOP TIPS

- Some of these areas are large and you will probably be able to find lots of information.
- Don't try to use it all!
- Sort and select what you think is the most useful to show that you understand about your chosen area, and use only that.
- This piece of work should not be huge!! You are *not* writing a book!

The example that follows gives you ideas for *one* way of organising your research using **play** as a BAR. It is not the only way it could be done.

➡ AN EXAMPLE OF A BAR AND FAR

BAR – PLAY

Children learn through play. This is a large topic and you should be able to find lots of information about it for your background research.

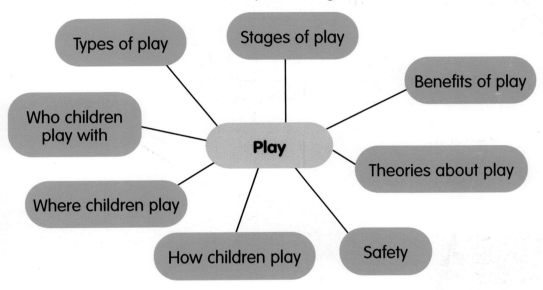

For your background research into play you could find out information about some or all of these suggestions. You may also be able to think of others.

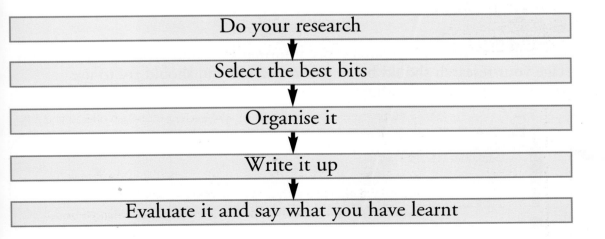

From this information you should now be able to choose a smaller area which is easier to manage. This will be your **focused area of research (FAR)**. For example, you might choose **types of play** as your FAR.

State what FAR you have chosen and explain (give reasons) why you have made your choice, remembering to link it to the child you are studying.

FAR – TYPES OF PLAY

From your background research you might choose to look more closely at *some* of the ideas below.

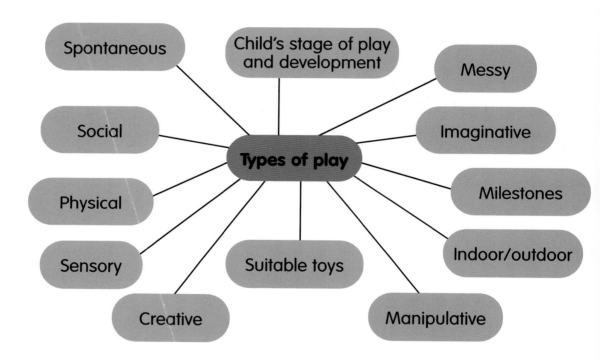

You will now need to research more information about types of play. At this stage your research should be *more detailed* and you should try to use **primary** as well as **secondary** sources.

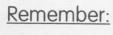

Remember:

It is very important to focus your research on the age and stage of development of the child you are studying!

Select and sort your information carefully and try to present it in different ways (see p. 7).

NOW:

Think about *what* you have learnt and *how* you can use it when planning your visits.

Remember:

The main aim of your child study visits is to look at your child's physical, intellectual, emotional and social development (PIES).

TOP TIPS

It is important to show that what you choose to do in your visits *links* with your research *and* the child you are studying.

To do this you must give a simple prediction/hypothesis of what you are going to try to prove or disprove.
e.g.

'Amy's parents understand the importance of different types of play and try to give her lots of opportunities to play in different ways.'

Or

'Josh prefers to play more with his toys indoors than to play outdoors. I think this will mean that his fine motor skills are developing faster than his gross motor skills.'

Or

'William has more chances to do creative and imaginative play at nursery than at home. This is because these types of play are more difficult to organise.'

Once you have done this you can plan your visits. You could use a simple planning sheet to show what you will be doing (see Appendix 5).

At least three of your visits should be based on your research. You could:

a) Plan activities.

Or

b) Carry out such things as:
- surveys;
- questionnaires;
- interviews;
- risk assessments and so on;

at the same time as your visit.

Or

c) Do a mixture of a and b.

Obviously what you choose to do will depend on what you hope to find out.

You may want to compare the value of three different types of play, e.g. creative, social and imaginative. You decide to do one visit on creative play, one on social and one on imaginative play. For each of these visits you could choose one or more of the activities suggested on page 45, e.g.:
- Creative play – a collage (made into a birthday card).
- Social play – a visit to a soft play area.
- Imaginative play – dressing up and making a den.

Remember:

There must be a simple *link* between your focused research and these activities/investigations.

To help you understand the importance of this, imagine a train with three carriages travelling along a track. To get safely from the start to the finish of the journey, the carriages must be securely *linked* to each other and to the engine.

In the same way, to get successfully from your focussed research to your final evaluation your three activities/investigations need to be linked to each other and the research.

SUGGESTIONS FOR FAR VISITS FOR TYPES OF PLAY

Activities

Creative play	Social play	Imaginative play
• Making a collage • Painting • Drawing • Modelling with salt dough/play dough • Making a card	• Tea party with other children • Board games which involve taking turns • Dressing up games • Any game which requires co-operation and sharing • Visiting a soft play area	• Dressing up • Small world • Making dens • Cooking • Puppet shows

Other suggestions for FAR visits

- Inventory of the toys/games that the child has for creative, social and imaginative play.
- Interview the parent/carer about the types of play the child enjoys, and how the parent/carer or other outside groups encourage the child to play.
- Visit the nursery that the child attends and observe an aspect of play.

The train below shows 3 ideas that link together for **types of play**. You could choose others.

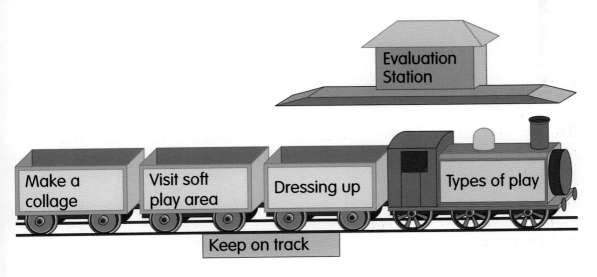

OTHER EXAMPLES OF FARS FOR PLAY

CHOSEN FAR – CREATIVE PLAY

From your background research into **play**, you might choose to look more closely at **creative play**.

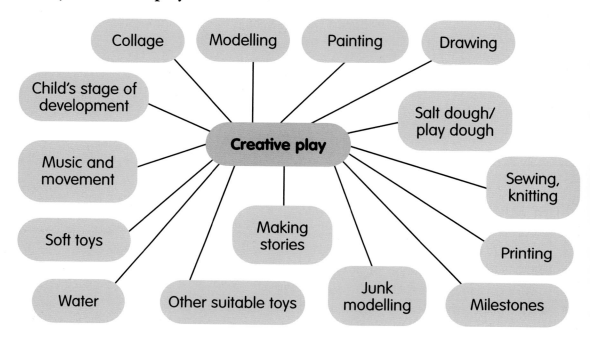

Once you have finished your research into **creative play**, use it to plan your visits (see pages 43 to 44).

SUGGESTIONS FOR FAR VISITS FOR CREATIVE PLAY

Activities

Painting, drawing and printing	Cutting and sticking	Junk modelling
• Finger painting • Block painting • Printing with hands and feet or fruit and vegetables • Dot-to-dot drawing	• Making a card for a special occasion • Making a mask • Mosaics from old coloured magazines	• Animals from a cereal box • Doll's house from a shoe box • Car from a large cardboard box

Other suggestions for FAR visits

- Inventory of the materials available at home which encourage creative play.
- Questionnaire for the child's nursery to find out from the staff what creative activities the child is involved in and enjoys.
- Interview the parent/carer about how they encourage creative play.

You may have decided to look at painting, drawing and printing for your FAR visits (see pages 65 to 74).

The train below shows 3 ideas that link these together for **creative play**. You could choose others.

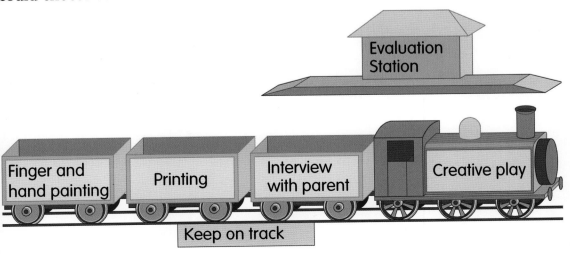

CHOSEN FAR – MANIPULATIVE PLAY

From your background research into **play**, you might choose to look more closely at **manipulative play**.

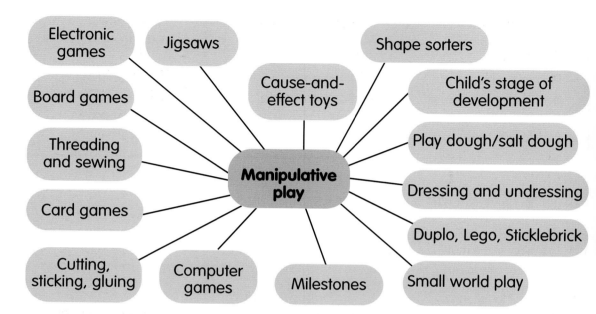

Once you have finished your research into **manipulative play**, use it to plan your visits (see pages 43 to 44).

SUGGESTIONS FOR FAR VISITS FOR MANIPULATIVE PLAY

Activities

Construction toys	Small world play	Keyboards

• Observing the child playing with:
   • Duplo
   • Lego
   • Sticklebricks
 • Creating their own models from junk
 • K'nex
	• Trains
	 • Playmobile
	 • Doll's house
	 • Zoo/farm animals
		• Musical instruments
		 • Electronic games
		 • Computer games/ CD-Roms

Other suggestions for FAR visits

- Interview the parents about the child's manipulative skills, how they are encouraged etc.
- Visit the nursery to observe the child's different types of manipulative play or interview staff about this.
- Inventory of the toys at home and how they encourage manipulative play.

The train below shows 3 ideas that link together for **manipulative play**. You could choose others.

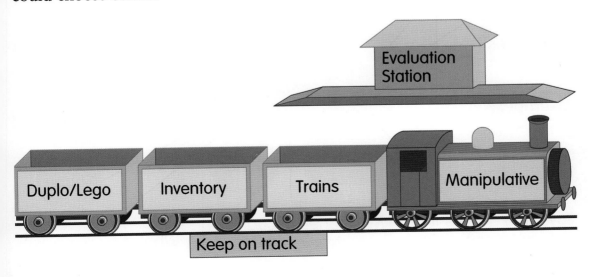

➡ FURTHER EXAMPLES OF BARS AND FARS

BAR – INTELLECTUAL DEVELOPMENT

The following pages give further ideas for:
- ✏ intellectual development;
- ✏ healthy eating;
- ✏ music and movement;
- ✏ pre-school groups;
- ✏ safety.

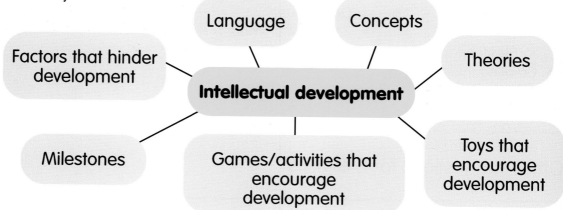

CHOSEN FAR – CONCEPTS

From your background research into **intellectual development** you might choose to look more closely at **concepts**.

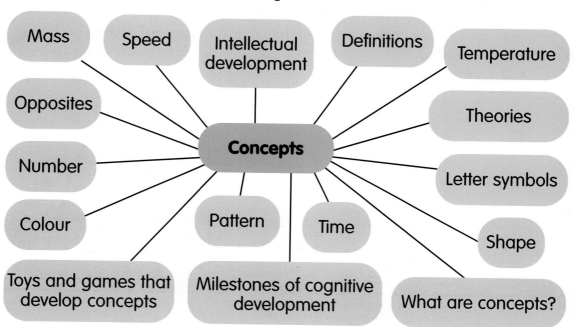

Once you have finished your research into **concepts** use it to plan your visits (see pages 43 to 44)

SUGGESTIONS FOR FAR VISITS FOR CONCEPTS
Activity

Number	Shape	Colour
• Songs and rhymes, e.g. 'ten green bottles', 'round and round the garden' • Playing board games using dice • Playing dominoes • Shopping games • Designing an activity book e.g. dot-to-dot	• Playing with shapes sorters with very young children • Using play/salt dough to roll and cut out shapes • Making and copying 3D shapes • Reading a book together about shapes • Looking at the shapes of everyday objects	• Painting and mixing colours • Painting by numbers • Reading a book about colours

Other suggestions for FAR visits

- Inventory of child's books and games to see how they encourage concepts.
- Interview the parents/carers about the way in which they help the child to develop a concept/concepts.
- Make a simple game or book about concepts to use with your child.

The train below shows 3 ideas that link together for the **concepts** of number, shape and colour. You could choose other concepts and/or ideas.

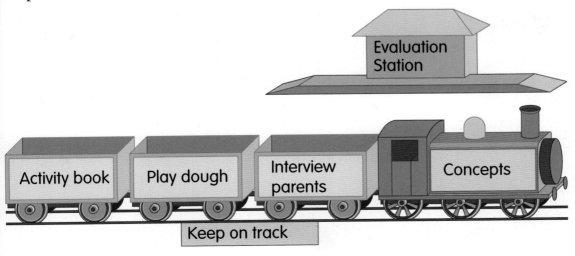

CHOSEN FAR – LANGUAGE

From your background research into **intellectual development** you might choose to look more closely at **language**.

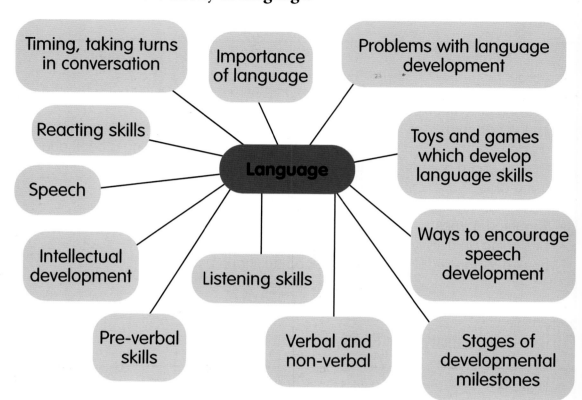

Once you have finished your research into **language**, use it to plan your visits (see pages 43 to 44)

SUGGESTIONS FOR FAR VISITS FOR LANGUAGE DEVELOPMENT

Activities

Songs and rhymes	Pretend play	Books
• Action songs • Singalong tapes, CDs • Nursery rhymes • Poetry	• Small world play e.g. hospital, school, farm • Making a car from a cardboard box and using it to visit the seaside • Making a play or story using puppets and performing to friends or family • Playing at cafes, waiting on a serving	• Interactive • Talking • Flapbooks • Making books • Reading

Other suggestions for FAR visits

- Interview the parents/carer about the ways in which they encourage the child's language to develop.
- Visit the child's nursery and interview the supervisor about the child's language development.
- Comparison – choose a selection of the child's books/toys and investigate how they encourage language skills.

The train below shows 3 ideas that link together for **language**. You could choose others.

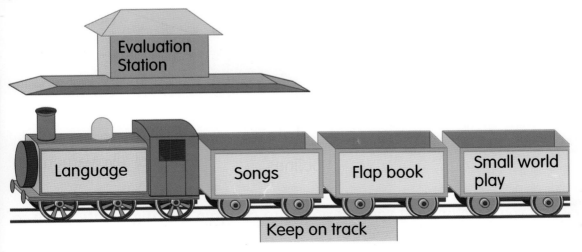

BAR – HEALTHY EATING

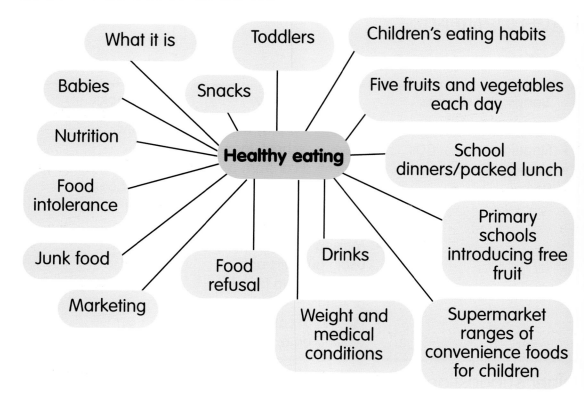

What it is

Toddlers

Children's eating habits

Babies

Snacks

Five fruits and vegetables each day

Nutrition

Healthy eating

School dinners/packed lunch

Food intolerance

Junk food

Food refusal

Drinks

Primary schools introducing free fruit

Marketing

Weight and medical conditions

Supermarket ranges of convenience foods for children

CHOSEN FAR – CHILDREN'S EATING HABITS

From your background research into **healthy eating** you might choose to look more closely at **children's eating habits**.

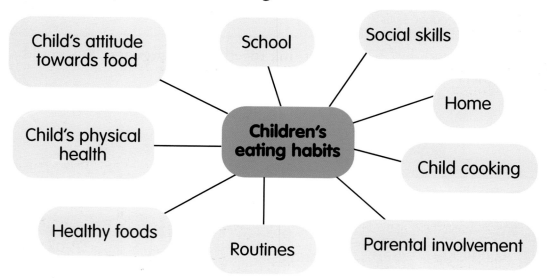

Child's attitude towards food

School

Social skills

Home

Child's physical health

Children's eating habits

Child cooking

Healthy foods

Routines

Parental involvement

Once you have finished your research into **children's eating habits**, use it to plan your visits (see pages 43 to 44)

SUGGESTIONS FOR FAR VISITS FOR CHILDREN'S EATING HABITS

Activities

Social skills	Making healthy food/meals	Encouraging healthy eating
• Tea parties • Children's parties • Meal times • Eating habits	• Baking bread • Preparing a healthy snack • Making a smoothie drink with fruit and milk	• Making a book about healthy food • Shopping trip to the supermarket to buy healthy food • Eating plate (see page 106)

Other suggestions for FAR visits

- Visit the child's school and investigate packed lunches, meals and snacks offered. Analyse how healthy the child's diet is.
- Interview the child/parents about the types of food the child likes to eat and about their meal time routines.
- Give a questionnaire to the parents about ways in which they encourage the child to eat more healthy foods.
- Conduct a survey – if watching children's TV programmes with your child, look at the number and type of adverts for food or drinks.

The train below shows 3 ideas that link together for **children's eating habits**. You could choose others.

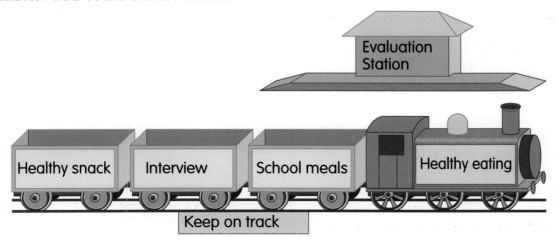

> **Remember:**
> Ask parents about food allergies or other dietary restrictions your child may have.

BAR – MUSIC AND MOVEMENT

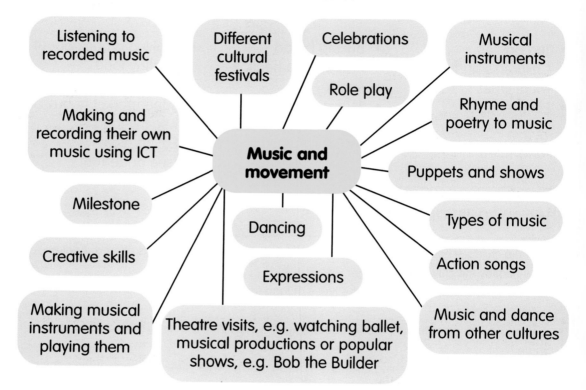

CHOSEN FAR – MAKING MUSIC

From your background research into **music and movement** you might choose to look more closely at **making music**.

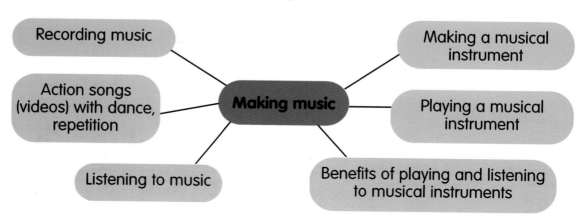

Once you have finished your research into **making music**, use it to plan your visits (see pages 43 to 44)

SUGGESTIONS FOR FAR VISITS FOR MAKING MUSIC

Activities

Making music	Playing a musical instrument	Dance
• Making musical intruments from household products • Using musical instruments to produce sounds to the rhythm of the music • Performing a song to a parent/sibling • Recording the song on a tape recorder and listening to it	• Piano/keyboard • Drums • Recorder • Triangle	• Action songs to videos • Dancing to music • Ballet/tap • Gymnastics • Pop Idol

Other suggestions for FAR visits

- Visit a toy shop and investigate the toys/books which encourage listening/dancing/singing skills with the child/parent/carer.
- Inventory of the toys/games/activities that may encourage the child's interest in music, movement and dance at home.
- Interview the parent/carer about what the child likes/does not like about singing, dancing and making music.

The train below shows 3 ideas that link together for **making music**. You could choose others.

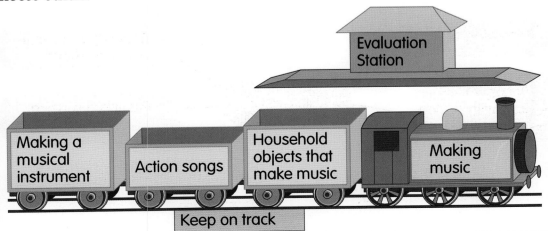

BAR – PRE-SCHOOL GROUPS

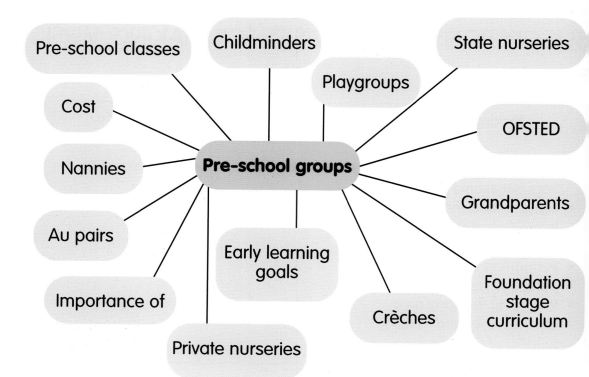

The child you are studying may go to a childminder and also attend a nursery one morning a week. This may help you to decide on your focused area of research.

CHOSEN FAR – CHILDMINDERS AND PRIVATE NURSERIES

From your background research into **pre-school groups** you might choose to look more closely at **childminders and private nurseries**.

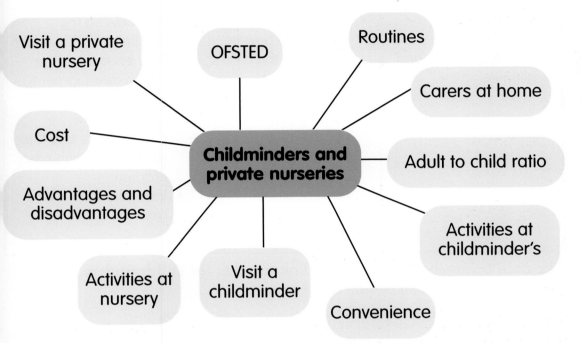

Once you have finished your research into **childminders and private nurseries**, use it to plan your visits (see pages 43 to 44).

> **Remember:**
>
> Trying to plan and carry out practical activities at a childminder's and/or nursery could be very difficult.
>
> Instead, you may find it easier to carry out some of the following suggestions.

SUGGESTIONS FOR FAR VISITS FOR CHILDMINDERS AND PRIVATE NURSERIES

Activities

Parents/carers	Private nursery	Childminders
• Interviewing the parent/carer • Inventory of toys and activities	• Visiting the nursery to investigate how it influences the child's development • Interviewing the nursery supervisor about how to encourage children's development at nursery school • Inventory of toys and activities	• Interviewing the childminder about how they encourage the child's development • Observing the child playing at the childminders and their relationship with other children • Inventory of toys and activities

The train below shows 3 ideas that link together for **childminders and private nurseries**. You could choose others.

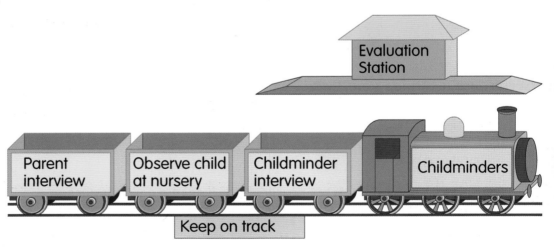

Safety
- Laws/regulations
- In the home
- Risk assessment
- Equipment
- Water
- First aid
- Garden/pond
- Sun
- Supervision of games
- Accident prevention
- Outdoor
- Toys

CHOSEN FAR – SAFETY OF TOYS

Safety with toys and at play
- Choosing suitable toys for the age range
- Trading Standards
- Toy Safety Regulations 1995
- Playing safely
- Risk assessment
- Safety marks e.g. the Kite mark
- Toy manufacturer's advice
- Checking and maintaining toys

Once you have finished your research into **safety of toys**, use it to plan your visits (see pages 43 to 44).

> ## ! Remember:
>
> Planning activities to look at safety must be done very carefully. You must at no time deliberatley put your child in a dangerous situation. Instead look at some of the suggestions below for activities/investigations.

SUGGESTIONS FOR FAR VISITS FOR SAFETY OF TOYS

Investigations	Activities
• Doing an inventory of the child's indoor and outdoor toys, e.g. look at: i) safety features/symbols ii) hygiene iii) manufacturer's instructions iv) overall condition of the toys v) suitability for the child's age • Interviewing parents about toy safety • Carrying out a risk assessment when playing indoors/outdoors with toys	• Small world play to enhance safety awareness • Making a book with the child about how to prevent accidents e.g. when playing outside with animals • Role-play games e.g. safety near water or on the roads

The train below shows 3 ideas that link together for **safety of toys**. You could choose others.

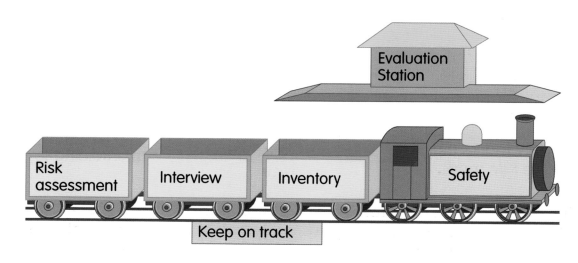

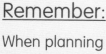

Remember:

When planning visits or visiting your child you are not expected to have sole responsibility for the child.

Practical activities and investigations

In this section we will look at ideas for activities/investigations that could be planned for your child study visits, and how they might help physical, intellectual, emotional and social development.

Before planning your visit it might be helpful to remember that children are often cared for by people other than their parents before they reach the age that they have to start school.

Children may go to one or more of the following:
- childminder;
- nanny;
- playgroup;
- nursery school;
- nursery class;
- crèche;
- private nurseries;
- pre-school;
- daycare setting.

The Foundation Stage Curriculum Framework has been developed to help children reach the early learning goals ready for entry year 1 at school. You can get a copy of this from www.qca.org.uk/ages3-14/160.html

There are six areas of learning:

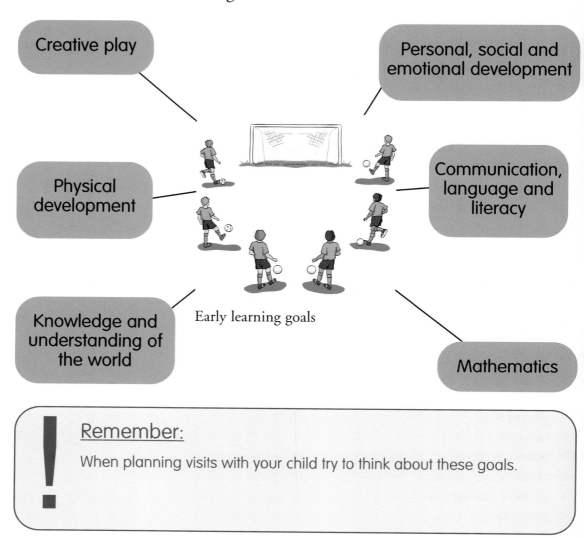

Creative play

Personal, social and emotional development

Physical development

Communication, language and literacy

Knowledge and understanding of the world

Early learning goals

Mathematics

> ! **Remember:**
>
> When planning visits with your child try to think about these goals.

➡ CREATIVE PLAY AND ACTIVITIES

WHAT IS CREATIVE PLAY?

Creative play takes place when children use different materials to make something from their own ideas and imagination.

It lets them explore and experiment with different materials, use their senses to find out what can and cannot be done and express their own ideas and feelings about the world they live in.

The end result may not be recognisable and the child may not even want to keep it! It is important, however, that what they make is praised and not made fun of.

Creative play can help all areas of development including:
- physical skills and co-ordination;
- language skills;
- understanding ideas and concepts;
- working with others;
- confidence, independence and self-esteem.

PAINTING, DRAWING AND PRINTING

As soon as young children can hold crayons in a palmar grasp, they will enjoy making marks on paper.

Painting, printing and drawing are great activities for children of all ages. They can help all areas of development and are great fun. If you plan a painting activity as part of your study or research you will be able to find out a lot about the child's development, give the child a lot of pleasure by creating a 'work of art' (even though you might not be able to tell what it is!) and have lots of fun.

> ## Remember:
> Before planning activities check out the stages of development of drawing skills.

15 months	• May grasp a crayon using a palmar grasp. • Will use a crayon to scribble backwards and forward.
18 months	• May hold a crayon with a primitive tripod grasp. • Beginning to show a preference for right or left hand.
2–2½ years	• Tries to hold a pencil close to the point in a primitive tripod grasp. • May make letters V and T. • Beginning to make circular scribbles and lift hand off paper to make lines.
3–3½ years	• Has quite good control of pencil between thumb and first two fingers. • Can draw circles, squares, lines, dots etc. • Draws people, and a head with one or two features. • May talk about drawings before starting.
4–5 years	• Begins to add more details and uses more colour. • Drawings are more complex and varied. • Pictures will have more background. • Will draw houses with doors, windows etc., trees, cars. • Can colour neatly.

PLANNING AND ORGANISING

As with any activity, making the right choice and planning it carefully will make the experience more successful – for the child and for you. Look at the different ideas shown below.

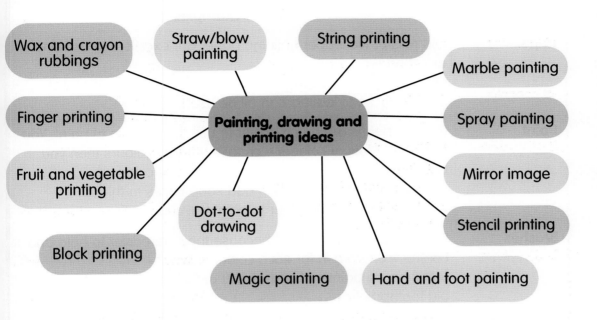

Wax and crayon rubbings

Straw/blow painting

String printing

Marble painting

Finger printing

Painting, drawing and printing ideas

Spray painting

Fruit and vegetable printing

Mirror image

Dot-to-dot drawing

Stencil printing

Block printing

Magic painting

Hand and foot painting

Think About

The activities you choose must be:
- suitable for the age of the child you are studying (check the development charts in Section 6;
- enough to keep the child interested and excited (children have a low attention span, especially younger children, so two or three different ideas may need to be planned).

Once you have chosen what to do:

Think About

- What materials you will need and where to get them.
- Where you will set up the activity.
- Covering the work surface or floor – layers of newspaper or cheap plastic sheeting from a garden centre are good.
- The amount of space you will need.
- How you will dry the paintings.
- Somewhere to wash and dry hands as you work.
- Wearing old clothes.
- Safety – non-toxic paints, non-sharp equipment.

WHAT ABOUT MATERIALS?

Materials for painting and printing can be expensive – but with a little thought and imagination you will probably be able to use things from around the home to produce exciting and different effects.

Material	Ideas, Examples
Paper	Old rolls of wallpaper or lining paper are excellent to use and are cheap. Old/used computer paper, backs of cards, insides of cereal boxes, backs of leaflets can all be used.
Paint	Powder paints are much easier to use than blocks of paint. You don't need lots of colours – choose primary colours then you can experiment with mixing to create 'new' colours. Thick paint is best – you can add soap flakes to thicken it. Adding sand, salt or sugar to paint will change the texture.
Brushes	Short fat brushes are best because they are easier to hold and control – one brush for each colour is best. Small house painting brushes (2½ or 3½ cm) are good, as are old toothbrushes.
Things other than brushes	Be adventurous! Try using cotton buds, twigs, feathers. . . . They will all make interesting and different marks.
Pots and palettes	You will need a pot for each colour paint. Try to use containers which will not knock over easily, e.g. margarine tubs, yogurt cartons, plastic egg boxes. Beware of jam jars – if knocked over they can break.
Pens and crayons	Try to provide a variety of different types and thicknesses so the child can experiment – such as wax crayons, charcoal, plastic crayons, chalk, ordinary and coloured pencils. Even try felt tip pens, as long as they are non-toxic and impermanent.
Printing	Potatoes and turnips are good for cutting out shapes (you will need to do the cutting). You could also use fruit and vegetables such as celery, carrots, leeks, apples, peppers. If this seems wasteful look around at home and you will find lots you could use – cotton reels, thimbles, sponges, clothes-pegs, balloons, corrugated paper, bubble wrap, pasta shapes, combs, biscuit cutters and so on.

HOW PAINTING, DRAWING AND PRINTING CAN HELP LEARNING AND DEVELOPMENT

Physical development
- Using crayons, pens, brushes, etc. can help develop fine motor skills, hand–eye co-ordination and handling and control.
- Painting at an easel or doing foot/hand prints can help gross motor skills.
- All of these activities can develop sensory skills, especially sight and touch.

Intellectual – concepts
- Using colours, textures, shapes and space will help to develop creativity.
- Painting, drawing and printing will help develop the imagination.
- Mixing colours together or adding, sand or salt to change the texture helps to understand cause and effect.
- All of these activities can help to develop concentration and memory.

Intellectual – language
- Children will enjoy talking about their drawings and paintings.
- They will be encouraged to ask questions, listen and follow instructions.
- They will learn new words about painting and drawing.

Social development
- Taking turns.
- Co-operating.
- Self control.
- Listening to instructions.

Emotional development
- All these activities allow children to experience both positive and negative emotions, e.g. pride, excitement, frustration, happiness.
- They can increase children's confidence and self-esteem.
- They encourage independence.
- They allow children to make choices and paint how they feel.

Other areas
- Numeracy – using and understanding numbers, sizes, shapes, repeats, patterns, sequences.
- Understanding of the world – looking at objects, flowers, animals, insects, using science and nature for ideas.

SOME IDEAS FOR PAINTING, PRINTING AND DRAWING

Remember:

Choose an activity or a range of activities you think the child will enjoy and be able to do. Choosing something difficult will possibly end in tears and tantrums!

Finger painting

You will need

- Powder paint
- Wallpaper paste (non-fungicide)
- An easy-clean surface or large tray

What to do

- Make up the paint with wallpaper paste to a thick consistency.
- Pour it onto a work surface or plastic tray.
- Let the child make patterns and shapes using their hands and fingers.

You could also:

- Talk about the touch, feel and texture of the paint, introducing new words.
- Make hand prints onto paper.

Finger painting

Printing

You will need

- Saucer with different coloured paints
- Potatoes
- Paper

What to do

- Cut the potato in half.
- Cut a different design onto each half.
- Dip the potato into the saucer of paint.
- Stamp onto a clean sheet of paper.

You could also:

- Rotate the print to make different patterns or use alternate colours.
- Use cut fruits and vegetables, bobbins, clothes pegs (see page 68).
- Use sponges and experiment with thinner/thicker paints.

Potato painting

Blow/straw painting

You will need

- Straws
- Paper
- Thin paint

What to do

- Drizzle blobs of runny paint onto paper.
- Blow through straws in different directions to make patterns.
- Try with different colours.

Straw painting

Pencil or wax rubbings

You will need

- Paper
- Wax crayon or coloured pencils
- Coins or leaves

What to do

- Put the coin or leaf under the sheet of paper. Gently rub over the top with a crayon or pencil.

You could also

- Use bark or embossed cards.

Wax rubbing

Mirror-image painting

You will need
- Paper
- Brushes
- Coloured paint

What to do
- Fold a piece of paper in half and open out.
- Use the brush to drop blobs of coloured paint onto one half.
- Fold over the other half of the paper again and smooth with your hand.
- Open out to see the pattern.

Magic painting

You will need
- Paper
- A white wax candle
- Paint
- Brushes

What to do
- Draw a picture or a message on to a sheet of paper using the candle.
- Get the child to paint over the paper to reveal the picture or message.

Drawing

Drawing activities do not take as much organising as painting, and are usually not as messy, but they do need to be planned!

Drawing has to be learnt – and it takes time. How good children become will depend partly on whether they have natural ability, and partly on whether they are given plenty of chances to practise and enjoy drawing.

Early 'drawings' will just be scribbles so do not expect anything you can recognise until the child is about 3 years old! Check in textbooks and Section 6 (Development of the child) before planning.

Drawing

Some ideas

- Use bought colouring books – this will help to develop fine motor skills and hand eye co-ordination. It takes a lot of skill to keep inside the lines.
- Make your own dot-to-dot drawings of familiar things, e.g. flowers, balls, cars, houses.
- Draw around everyday objects like stencils, wooden bricks, jigsaw puzzle pieces and even hands. You could then make faces or other objects out of them or colour them in.
- With older children do simple drawings and get the child to colour them in.

➡ COLLAGES – AND OTHER CUTTING AND STICKING ACTIVITIES

A collage is a creative activity, where scraps of paper, fabric, photographs, string, twigs, leaves, foil, etc. are stuck onto a background. Like painting, drawing and printing, making a collage is a messy activity, which most children will enjoy. It is also an activity that will help all areas of development.

Collages can be quite simple and small – such as a birthday card. They can be much larger and more detailed than this, such as a picture of a day at the beach or a farmyard scene, and may also involve painting and printing. These can be quite difficult and take a lot of time, patience, concentration and skills.

PLANNING AND ORGANISING

If you try to do something like this with a young child, they will quickly become bored and very frustrated – so when planning these sorts of activities you must think about what skills your child has.

Cutting out is difficult – it means that children have to learn to use and co-ordinate their hand and finger movements in a totally new way – to snip. Once they have learnt to do this they then have to plan where to cut and guide the scissors in the right direction. Even adults can have problems with this! Tearing paper into strips and shapes is just as exciting for young children and not as frustrating.

Gluing and sticking are also difficult – trying to put the glue where it is needed requires a lot of skill, as does positioning it onto the background in the right place.

So don't expect too much – even a five-year-old may not be able to cut out and glue accurately.

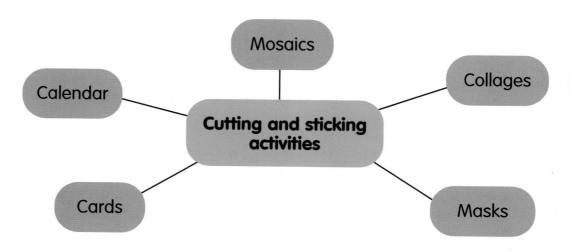

Remember:

Make sure you choose something which is suitable for the age and interest of the child – and their level of development!

2–2½-years-old	• Children will enjoy ripping paper into strips. • May be able to snip narrow paper with plastic scissors. • Can spread glue but will need a lot of help. • Can drop things onto a glued surface to stick into place.
2½–3-years-old	• Should be able to snip paper confidently. • Can spread glue, if helped.
3½–4-years-old	• Can rip around pictures. • Can spread glue more carefully. • Can put glue onto the back of 'ripped out' shapes. • .May begin to use scissors to cut out shapes.
4½–5-years-old	• Cutting skills are better but still not accurate. • May begin to 'arrange' pictures.

Think About

- Decide on a suitable area to work at and make sure surfaces are protected.
- Try to have somewhere nearby to wash hands.
- Have a good range of materials to work with – but do not give them all at once.
- Make sure you have everything you need before you start.
- Try to have an idea of what to make before you start.
- With an older child (4–5) talk to them about what you could do so they will feel more grown up and be more interested.
- When working with the child do not 'take over' and do everything for them.
- **Remember health and safety – make sure all glues, paints etc. are non-toxic, supervise all the time and if using scissors, use blunt-ended ones.**

What about materials?

Paper and card
Tissue paper, coloured paper and card, newspaper, magazines, catalogues, leaflets, wallpaper, wrapping paper, crepe paper, birthday or Christmas cards

Fabrics
Scraps of materials with different textures, e.g. wool, silk, satin, leather. Knitting wools, embroidery threads, feathers, cotton wool balls and string

Use with care
Sequins, glitter, sands, rice, dried beans, peas, pasta

Natural materials
Leaves, stones, twigs, shells, corks, pieces of bark from trees, wood shavings, sand, flowers

Glues
Glue sticks are good for gluing paper to paper or even lightweight fabrics to paper; but they can be hard to control.

PVA glue is strong and will go transparent when it dries. You can use brushes or spatulas with it which are easier for children to handle.

Wallpaper paste is cheap and good for sticking paper to paper. It can be used with a brush, making it easier for children to control.

> **Remember:**
> * Choose a variety of materials which are suitable for the activity you have planned.
> * Provide only a small selection of materials – about 6–8 – otherwise the child will be confused about what to use.

HOW CUTTING AND STICKING CAN HELP DEVELOPMENT

Physical
Tearing, cutting and sticking will help children:
* develop gross motor skills – arm muscles;
* develop and improve fine motor skills;
* develop hand–eye co-ordination;
* become skilful at using other small hand-held tools.

Handling different materials will help to develop sensory skills.

Intellectual – concepts
These activities will help children:
* learn about and use new and different materials in different ways;
* develop decision-making and problem-solving skills when deciding what to do and how to do it;
* develop an understanding of concepts such as colour, size, shape, number, etc.;
* develop their imagination and creativity.

Intellectual – language
* Will improve and increase vocabulary – words of materials and tools and descriptive words.
* Improve language skills by asking questions and following instructions.

Social
* Learning to work with others.
* Sharing and co-operating.
* Communicating and following instructions.

Emotional
* Children will be able to experience positive emotions – pleasure, pride, contentment, happiness.
* Could begin to learn to control frustration and anger.
* Will encourage patience and concentration.
* Will improve confidence and self-esteem.

Other areas
Numeracy – sizes and shapes, making patterns, estimating amount, counting, use of space.
Art – learning to appreciate colour, shape, textures.

SOME IDEAS FOR ACTIVITIES

Making cards

Cards can be made for all sorts of occasions (e.g. birthday, Christmas, Mother's Day, get well cards). The same ideas can be used to make party invitations.

Some ideas
- You could use a computer to help the child to write a message for inside the card.
- Cut out and stick on pictures from old birthday or Christmas cards.
- Draw a picture of a simple shape (e.g. a flower, a boat, balloons). Scrunch up small pieces of tissue paper and stick inside the shapes.
- Cut simple shapes out of a piece of card and stick tissue paper or cellophane behind to give a stained glass window effect.

Making masks

Children love making and wearing masks – either of people or animals, birds, etc. They can be decorated with fabric, feathers, coloured tissue paper, foil, sequins, etc. Detail can be added with paints and crayons.

Face masks made from paper

Wool or fabric can be used for hair. They can be used in imaginative play.

- Make the basic shape out of card – roll it into a tube first so it will fit the shape of the head more easily.
- Make holes in each side, thread elastic through and fasten.
- Cut out eye holes and perhaps nose and mouth holes.
- Decorate.

You could also make masks from paper plates (not paper bags).

Mosaics

Mosaics are made by cutting or tearing small pieces of coloured paper and sticking them onto paper to make a pattern or shape.

Tissue paper is good for this because it can be scrunched up into balls and then stuck down. This gives a 3-D effect.

- Cut or tear up pieces of paper and sort into colours (this will encourage sorting skills and colour recognition).
- Draw a simple pattern or a simple shape onto card or paper, for example, a flower, a clown, a sheep, a boat.

✏ Decide on the colours to use.
✏ Stick the coloured paper onto the background to make the mosaic.

Children sticking paper mosaic tiles to simple shapes

Collages

> ! **Remember:**
>
> Making a collage will take quite a lot of time and patience!

Choose what you are going to make first – it might be an idea to find out what the child would like to do, but have some ideas yourself.

Possible ideas include: field with trees and sheep, house and garden, beach with boats, umbrellas and sandcastles, mountains and snow.
✏ Use a fairly large piece of card for the background.
✏ Use coloured card for the background wherever possible – otherwise try painting it.
✏ Sketch out a simple design onto the background.

✏ Once the child starts cutting and sticking, give advice and help only when needed.

A collage using coloured strips of paper

Making snowflakes

Once children can use scissors fairly accurately to snip, they will enjoy making snowflakes. Use different coloured tissue paper so that it is easy for them to cut.
✏ Cut out fairly large circles – use a plate as a guide.
✏ Fold the circle in half, then in half again, and then again.
✏ Snip small pieces out of each side.
✏ Open out to form the 'snowflake'.

These could then be stuck on to a larger piece of card and you could add a frame to make a picture.

MODELLING WITH PLAY DOUGH, SALT DOUGH AND PAPIER MÂCHÉ

Children of all ages enjoy making shapes (modelling) from materials such as play dough and salt dough. Younger children will just enjoy feeling, squeezing and stretching them into different shapes. Older children can use different tools to help shape the dough, such as blunt knives or shape cutters. Patterns can be stamped on the dough using forks, cotton reels, stampers, etc.

PLANNING AND ORGANISING

Quite young children will enjoy this sort of activity – those as young as 18 months to 2 years can squeeze and stretch the dough *provided* they have passed the 'mouthing' stage (putting everything into their mouths).

Remember:

- Don't expect too much of children. They may not be able to make a shape or object that you can recognise until they are about 4 or 5!
- Modelling is a messy activity.

18 months–2½ years old	<ul><li>Will enjoy handling and squeezing dough</li><li>May be able to copy making a sausage shape</li><li>May be able to decorate a piece of dough with different marks, if shown</li></ul>
3–4 years old	<ul><li>May begin to roll out, cut and make simple shapes</li><li>Handling and squeezing the dough is probably still more important than making shapes</li></ul>
4–5 years old	<ul><li>Will be able to make things such as bowls and snakes</li><li>Will enjoy using different objects to make marks on the dough</li></ul>

☺ Think About

- ✎ Where you will do it.
- ✎ Covering work surfaces.
- ✎ Wearing protective clothing.
- ✎ Safety.

HOW MODELLING CAN HELP DEVELOPMENT

Physical
Rolling, squashing, squeezing, pinching, shaping the dough will:
- strengthen arm muscles and fingers;
- improve fine motor skills;
- improve hand–eye co-ordination;
- teach how to use different tools and equipment correctly.

Sensory
Develops sensory skills of:
- touch
- sight
- smell.

Intellectual – concepts
- Learn about different shapes and sizes when making shapes.
- Learn to use their imagination.
- Learn to develop creative skills.
- Learn about the difference between materials.
- Learn about the properties of materials.

Intellectual – language
- Learn new words to describe colour, texture, shapes etc.
- Will enjoy talking about what they are doing.
- Ask questions.

Social
- Children often like to do this sort of activity on their own.
- Learning to accept safety and hygiene rules.

Emotional
- Rolling, squeezing, punching and shaping can all help to get rid of aggression (negative emotions).
- Will have fun and enjoy themselves.
- May feel good about what they have made – improve self confidence and self-esteem.
- May feel more independent.
- Can be relaxing.

Other areas
Numeracy
- Using numbers to count
- Understanding shapes
- Making patterns
- Size

Materials
- Learning that different materials have different properties.

You can buy play dough and other modelling materials – but it can be expensive. It is cheap and easy to make your own.

Play dough

This is a basic recipe that can be used for all sorts of modelling activities. If stored correctly it will keep for several weeks.

100 g plain flour 50 g salt 1 teaspoon cream of tartar 1 teaspoon oil 150 ml water 1–2 teaspoons food colouring	1. Put flour, salt and cream of tartar into a bowl. Add oil and food colouring to the water. 2. Gradually add the water to the dry ingredients – beat well to remove any lumps. 3. Cook over a low heat, *stirring all the time* until dough forms a ball which leaves the sides of the pan clean. 4. Put onto a lightly floured flat surface to cool (soak pan!). 5. Knead until smooth and stretchy.

- Make up batches of different coloured doughs, e.g. blue, red, yellow, green.
- Add glitter to make the dough sparkle.
- Wrap in clingfilm if not using the dough straight away.
- Store by wrapping in clingfilm and keeping in an airtight container in a fridge.

Salt dough

This is similar to play dough, but it can be baked so that it goes hard (this can take a long time).

It can be painted and varnished to make it last.

100 g plain flour 50 g salt 80 ml water 1 teaspoon oil or glycerine	1. Put flour, salt and oil into a bowl. Add the water little by little to make a smooth, stretchy but not sticky dough. 2. Put onto a floured surface. Knead until smooth, then use to make models. 3. Bake models at 150°C/Gas mark 3 until firm (1½–2 hours depending on thickness). 4. Paint and varnish finished models.

IDEAS FOR MODELLING WITH PLAY DOUGH AND SALT DOUGH

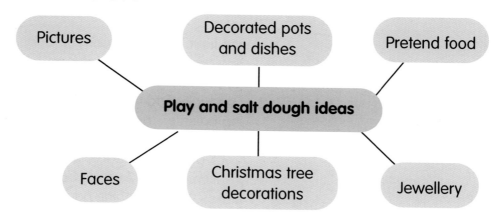

Pictures

Decorated pots and dishes

Pretend food

Play and salt dough ideas

Faces

Christmas tree decorations

Jewellery

➡ PAPIER MÂCHÉ

Papier mâché means 'mashed paper'. It is easy to make and can be used to create masks, bowls, plates, etc. which can then be painted and decorated.

You will need
- Lots of newspaper
- Flour and water paste or PVA glue mixed with water (1 part glue to 3 parts water)
- Paintbrushes
- Moulds – such as balloons, plates, bowls, plant pots
- Vaseline or clingfilm if using plates, bowls or plantpots

There are two ways to make papier mâché.

Method 1	Method 2
• Tear the paper into strips – about 2½ cm × 10 cm. • Put into a large bowl and cover with warm water. Leave to soak. • Squeeze out as much water as possible. • Mix paper together with glue to make a stiff consistency. • Spread a layer of the papier mâché over the mould. Press and smooth. Leave to dry. • Carefully remove mould and decorate with paints.	• Paste the strips of paper with glue using a paint brush. • Place the strips over the mould until covered with at least 3 layers. • Leave to dry. • Add 3 more layers and leave to dry. Repeat this until papier mâché is quite thick. • Carefully remove mould and decorate with paints.

- If using a balloon to make a head, the balloon can be 'popped' once the papier mâché is dry.
- If using plates, bowls or plant pots as moulds, cover with Vaseline or clingfilm to make it easier to remove.

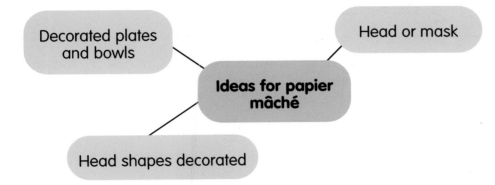

Decorated plates and bowls

Head or mask

Ideas for papier mâché

Head shapes decorated

➡ JUNK MODELLING

Children of all ages are fascinated by cardboard boxes and wrapping paper, and will play happily with them for hours. Younger children will use boxes as containers, and fill and empty them with bricks or other toys.

By the time children are 2½–3 years old they will be developed enough to be ready to try **junk modelling**. This is making models out of different household items such as empty cereal boxes or yoghurt cartons.

PLANNING AND ORGANISATION

Because junk modelling is similar to cutting and sticking and collage work, preparation and organisation for this activity is very much the same.

Creating a junk model

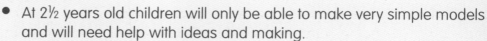

Remember:

- At 2½ years old children will only be able to make very simple models and will need help with ideas and making.
- By 3½–4 years old they will be more skilled and imaginative, will want to choose for themselves and be able to work more on their own – but will still need advice and support at times.

You need to collect a good range of junk materials (see below) and choose a suitable space for the activity.

Materials
Empty cereal boxes, biscuit boxes, shoe boxes, pizza boxes, kitchen roll tubes, egg boxes, yogurt cartons, margarine or butter containers
For sticking
PVA glue, brushes, sticky tape, string, paperclips, rubber bands, staples and split pins are best used only by adults
To decorate
Paints, crayons, tissue, felt pens, buttons, cotton wool balls, sequins, wool, pieces of fabric, glitter, etc.

HOW JUNK MODELLING CAN HELP DEVELOPMENT

Junk modelling helps learning and development in much the same way as cutting, sticking and collage making, and play dough modelling (see page 75).

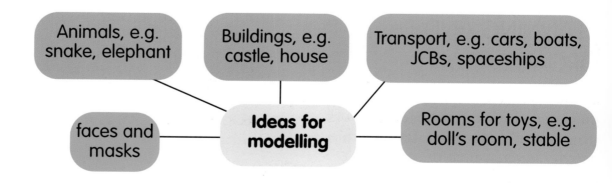

WHAT IS IMAGINATIVE PLAY?

Imaginative play is sometimes known as **pretend play**. It takes place when children act out being somebody or something else e.g. mum or dad, a robot, a tiger, a pop star.

Children learn by **copying** and **imitating** what they see and hear, and so often in this sort of play they use real-life situations that they may have seen, heard or experienced, and may pretend to be someone else. This is called **role play**.

Role play is important for children because it lets them use their imaginations to act out their own feelings and emotions, and also gives them a chance to experience other people's feelings when they take on different roles.

For imaginative play children may dress up for their part and use toys and everyday objects as 'props' in the story, e.g. a cardboard box may become a train, a space ship or a boat; their soft toys and teddies become the people in their stories.

STAGES OF IMAGINARY PLAY

Up to 18 months	Children will 'imitate' and copy adults' actions, e.g. waving goodbye, playing peek-a-boo.
18 months–2 years	Simple pretend play will start, usually involving favourite toys and dolls. Children will act out everyday situations, e.g. getting dressed, having tea, eating, going to bed.
2–2½ years	Children will take on other roles that they know, such as mum or dad. Then they will begin to include ideas from books, stories, TV programmes or videos that they have seen or heard but not experienced. This is often called **fantasy play**.
2½–3 years onwards	Children will enjoy imaginative play together and start to negotiate roles.

PLANNING AND ORGANISING

Imaginary play does not need expensive toys and needs little real planning because it depends on the child or children using their own ideas, imaginations and experiences. Parents and carers can only suggest ideas and then let the child develop them – if they want to!

What is more important is to have lots of things available for the child to use in this sort of play, that will 'fire' their imaginations, e.g.:
- a box of old clothes or lengths of fabric;
- accessories such as bags, hats, shoes or jewellery;

- small world play toys;
- cardboard boxes;
- sheets and old curtains;
- empty food packets, sweet and biscuit tins, boxes.

Then let the child's imagination take over.

Look at the ideas below.

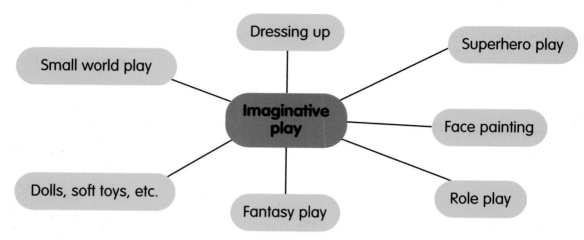

Think About

The activities you choose for imaginative play must be:
- suitable for the age and ability of the child you are studying – remember children have a short concentration span;
- supervised – if dressing up clothes are too big the child could trip and fall;
- fun for the child;

Once you have chosen what to do think about the following:
- what items of clothing or objects you will need to use;
- what items you may be able to borrow from parents;
- what other materials you might need;
- where the activity will take place;
- who will join in with the activity;
- using a book, story or video as an idea for the activity;

! Remember:

Safety
- Items that have sharp edges, or small items such as loose buttons that could cause choking, are not suitable for a child under the age of three years.
- If dressing up items are too big or long they could cause a child to trip.
- Cords, ties and belts could be dangerous if used by an unsupervised child, because they could accidentally strangle themselves.

WHAT RESOURCES WILL YOU NEED?

Children can play imaginatively without any specific equipment or resources. It is not necessary to go out and buy your child items to play with. For example, a large cardboard box can become a ship and old clothes can be used to dress up as a pirate.

HOW IMAGINATIVE PLAY CAN HELP LEARNING AND DEVELOPMENT

Physical
- Develops fine and gross motor skills when dressing up or making props for role play.
- Small world play will develop fine motor skills and hand–eye co-ordination.
- Imaginative play outdoors can develop gross motor skills, balance and co-ordination.
- Develops spatial awareness.

Social
When playing with other children it encourages:
- taking turns;
- sharing;
- co-operation;
- negotiating about roles, space, equipment;
- caring for others;
- respect for other people's ideas and feelings;
- solving problems together;
- making friends.

Emotional
Helps children to:
- experience and act out feelings e.g. sadness, enjoyment, frustration, anger, happiness;
- share and act out feelings that may be difficult to express;
- release tension and stress;
- build confidence and self-esteem;
- understand how other people feel;
- work through new or problem situations, e.g. moving house, going to the doctors/dentist, the arrival of a new baby.

Intellectual – concepts
- Helps to develop imagination and creativity when planning and making up stories and plays.
- Small world play helps to develop understanding of the world and how things work.
- Helps children to understand the concept of past, present and future.
- May help to develop maths and numeracy skills.
- Allows children to explore and experiment.
- Problem solving.

Intellectual – language
Children will
- learn new words;
- talk to themselves as they make up and act out stories;
- listen to and talk to other people as they play together;
- instruct others how to act out a certain role;
- re-tell known stories with small world play;
- re-tell their own stories with small world play.

➡ DRESSING UP

Children enjoy dressing up from an early age. Young children who may not be able to dress themselves can take part in simple role play with the help of an adult, e.g. by wearing a policeman's helmet.

Children could use any of the following to develop their imagination and role play:
- old clothing;
- accessories, e.g. hats, gloves, shoes;
- shop-bought outfits, including well-known characters e.g., Spiderman, Superman, Cinderella;
- jewellery - this could be an adult's old, unwanted junk jewellery or the child could make their own;
- props, e.g. a medical bag with a stethoscope;
- the child's own baby clothing used on their doll or teddy;
- face paints bought from specialist shops.

Children can play on their own or with a small group of children, and often without much help from adults. Children will develop their own characters and storylines in their role play.

Popular outfits

Many different well-known character outfits are worn and played with. This allows children to act out stories from books, videos and television programmes that they have watched.

Dressing dolls

Sometimes children like to dress their dolls and teddies in their own baby clothes then use them in role play stories.

A dressing up box

Children like to open a box full of dressing up clothes and choose an outfit. This allows a group of children to learn to share and agree over who should wear what. It also encourages their imagination.

Face painting

Specialist face paints can be used to develop a character or role. Children love to paint each others' faces when they get older.

> ## Remember:
>
> Face paints should conform to British Safety Standards. Always check with parents first to see if their child is allergic to the paints. A patch test could be done with a small amount of paint on the back of the hand before the paints are applied to the face.

➡ MAKING DENS

These can be made both inside and outside – if the weather is good and the area safe!

Making the den is one type of imaginative play – using it as a place to act out roles or stories or plan adventures is another. Dressing up may be part of the activity as well.

To make a den inside: tablecloths, towels, old sheets, old curtains etc. can be draped over chairs, clothes airers and furniture.
Toys and other accessories may then be moved inside the den or items made for the den from boxes, tins, etc.

When planning a den choose a corner of the room that is not in the way so that parents will allow the den to be kept for a while.

A den made from a rug and clothes airer

Outside dens can be made in the garden, again using old sheets, curtains, rugs or tablecloths draped over plastic garden furniture. They can also be made in gaps between bushes, in trees and in garden sheds, but parents must give permission and check that the area is safe.

An 'under-the-stairs' cupboard makes a great den but you must check with parents first and make sure that it is safe.

Children may also have shop-bought tents that make instant dens, e.g.:
- fairy castle;
- jungle;
- car;
- train;
- castle.

More expensive wooden chalets, traditional wendy houses and garden sheds also provide areas for children to develop their imagination. However, children often prefer the den that they have made themselves.

Children playing in a Wendy house

➡ USING CARDBOARD BOXES

Cardboard boxes can be used to develop imaginative play. The boxes are a cheap way of using a material that is no longer needed. The cardboard is usually strong, already in a box shape, sometimes with a lid, and comes in various sizes.

Types of cardboard boxes include cereal boxes, old shoe boxes, large cardboard boxes from a supermarket, etc.

SOME IDEAS

With a little imagination cardboard boxes can become many different things. Some ideas are given below.

Small boxes
- animals
- doll's house
- hotel
- secret garden
- miniature garden
- car for a teddy
- train for a doll
- shop till

Large boxes
- shop counter
- table for a tea party
- bed
- large doll's house
- kennel/stable
- boat/car/train

> **!** Remember:
> - Check for large staples that might hurt children.
> - Adults may need to help the child use scissors.

Children may want to develop these ideas further by painting the box to add more detail. The following materials could be used:

- safety scissors;
- paint/paintbrushes;
- glue/sticky tape;
- cotton reels;
- paper plates/cups;
- wool;
- foil paper/tissue paper;
- beads;
- dried flowers.

➡ USING HOUSEHOLD OBJECTS

Playing shops

To play shops, tins and small packets from the cupboard can be used, with parent's permission. A table cloth put over the top of a table is a simple way to display the goods. A till made from a shoe box with pretend money that the child has made, or a toy till with toy money, will make the shop more realistic. It may sell cakes, biscuits or crafts that you have made.

Puppets

Puppets made from socks

Puppets can be made from clean, old socks. Buttons, bands, felt tip pens and paint can be used for faces; wool for hair; and odd scraps of material for clothing. Socks and tights filled with sawdust make great heads for puppets. Shop-bought glove puppets, string puppets and finger puppets can also develop children's imagination. A home-made theatre could be made from a box.

Shadow puppets can be made cheaply with the use of a torch or bright light that can create patterns or images on the wall of a room and used to help make up stories at bedtime.

! Remember:
Toilet roll tubes may not be hygienic so try using kitchen roll tubes instead.

➡ DOLLS AND SOFT TOYS

Most children are bought lots of soft toys, animals, dolls and books, and often have large collections. They provide great emotional support and can form an important part of imaginative play. They can be used to act out the following situations.

birthday parties

the garage

the circus

the cafe

the zoo

the hospital

school or nursery

tea parties

the library

Tea and Birthday Parties

Children love to play at tea parties and birthday parties, sometimes with real food or just by pretending.

Children like to put real drinks into a cup and pretend that cold water is a hot drink.

Tea parties could take place on a small child's table with a miniature tea set. Teddies and dolls may be asked for tea or join in games and pretend to be at a party. A pretend birthday cake and candles can make the whole event more exciting.

The tea party or picnic could be a rug or towel placed into an imaginary field or the child's garden if the weather is fine.

SMALL WORLD PLAY

Small world play involves children playing with small characters and/or items. This type of play gives the child the opportunity to see a whole scene, for example a farm with animals, tractors, a field and fencing. The child may begin by creating part of the scene, such as a cow in a field, and then develop a more complicated scene with a storyline.

Toy shops sell a wide variety of small world play items, below are some examples:

Bought small world toys, e.g. garages, hospitals, space stations, zoos and shops, and the people who live in them, will give children hours of fun and lots of opportunities to make up stories and act out situations.

Children will often construct towns, buildings, cars, etc. from building bricks and construction toys such as Lego or Duplo, then use toys and toy cars to act out stories.

On a beach or in a garden, children will often build towns, castles, farms, houses and gardens by using sand or soil, and marking out roads and tracks.
Flowers and twigs will become trees, and pebbles can be people or cars.

Small world play with Tudor house, knights and horses

➡ FOOD AND COOKING

Preparing, cooking and, of course, eating food is an activity that children can enjoy from an early age – and one that can help many areas of development and learning.

Through handling food they can begin to understand about different countries and cultures, healthy eating, science and maths, weighing and measuring, hygiene and safety and how to be creative and imaginative etc. The list is endless and, of course, they get to eat the end product.

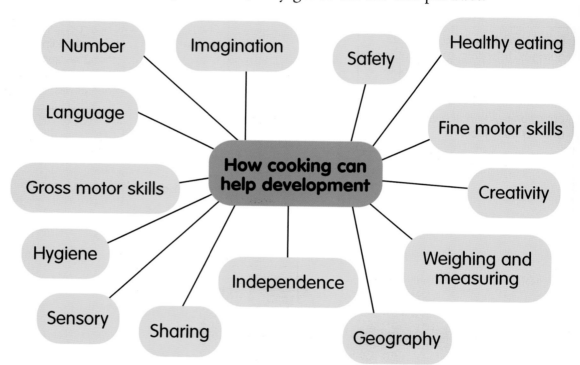

PLANNING AND ORGANISING

Don't think that food activities, and especially 'cooking', can only be done with older children. You do not always have to use an oven, microwave or sharp knives. With a little thought, imagination and careful planning, young children will get just as much fun and enjoyment out of making something that involves no cooking at all, as long as they are 'doing'. No child wants to sit and watch you do all the exciting bits!

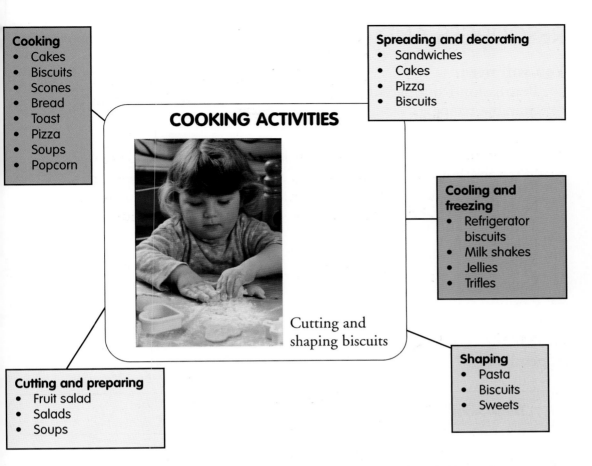

COOKING ACTIVITIES

Cooking
- Cakes
- Biscuits
- Scones
- Bread
- Toast
- Pizza
- Soups
- Popcorn

Spreading and decorating
- Sandwiches
- Cakes
- Pizza
- Biscuits

Cooling and freezing
- Refrigerator biscuits
- Milk shakes
- Jellies
- Trifles

Cutting and shaping biscuits

Shaping
- Pasta
- Biscuits
- Sweets

Cutting and preparing
- Fruit salad
- Salads
- Soups

Any food or cooking activity needs to be planned very carefully. Like any other activity you need to choose something which the child will enjoy, can succeed in and which will help their learning and development.

You must also think about **health and safety**.

Planning points	Yes	No
Is my choice too easy?		
Is my choice too difficult?		
Will my child enjoy it?		
Will it take too long?		
Is there plenty for my child to do?		
Have I thought about safety?		
Have I checked with the parents?		

RESOURCES AND PLANNING

You will need:
- Permission from parents
- Suitable recipe
- Ingredients
- Baking tray
- Oven gloves
- Rolling pin
- Non-breakable bowls
- Table, tea and wooden spoon
- Palette knife
- Apron
- Scales
- Cooling tray

Health and Safety: before you start, carry out a Risk Assessment (see Appendix 6).

 Think About

- Supervision
- Using and handling equipment
- Using the oven
- Protective clothing
- Possible allergies/dislike of foods
- Cleanliness
- Safe area for working
- Organising work area

HOW COOKING ACTIVITIES CAN HELP LEARNING AND DEVELOPMENT

Physical – gross motor skills
By:
- kneading bread mixtures;
- rolling out biscuits and pastry;
- beating and stirring cake mixtures;
- lifting ingredients to weigh out;
- pouring ingredients into bowls;
- cutting out shapes.

Physical – fine motor skills
By:
- measuring ingredients;
- weighing ingredients;
- spooning mixture into cases;
- cracking eggs into bowls;
- decorating cakes;
- cutting up fruit and vegetables;
- spreading fillings on bread or biscuits;
- icing cakes and biscuits;
- decorating pizzas;
- cutting out shapes for biscuits.

Sensory
- develops sensory skills of touch, smell and sight.

Social
- Learning to work with others.
- Sharing, taking turns and co-operating.
- Importance of hygiene and safety.
- Likes and dislikes.

Intellectual – concepts
Cooking activities can help develop concepts of:
- size;
- shape;
- number;
- weight;
- bigger/smaller;
- colour.

Intellectual – language
- New words for equipment and ingredients.
- Describing and comparing words.
- Asking questions and following instructions.
- Talking to others.
- Specialist words, e.g. creaming.

Emotional
- Gives opportunities to experience both positive and negative emotions.
- Helps to learn to control negative emotions, e.g. anger, frustration.
- Patience.

Other areas
Numeracy
- Volume, weight and measurement when weighing and measuring
- Sizes, e.g. bowls, spoons, cutters
- Shapes when cutting out
- Counting
- Comparing sizes and shapes
- Timing
- Estimating, e.g. when dividing mixtures into cases
Science
- Understanding solids and liquids
- How foods change when cooked or frozen
- Effect of heat
Health and safety
- Understanding safety rules
- Understanding hygiene rules

Children learn a lot by copying. It is sometimes a good idea to make the same dish as your child. That way you can work *alongside* them (a sort of parallel play) and show them what to do. This lets the child be more independent.

CHOOSING RECIPES

Recipes should be quite simple and easy to make. There should only be a few ingredients and not too many different stages. Recipe books written for children are a good place to look. Think about how long things will take to cook. Children are not always patient, so think about what you might do while the food is cooking. It might not always be safe or practical to do washing up!

Small cakes

These are quick and easy to make and cook. You could also add some cocoa, cherries or dried fruit to them.

Ingredients
100g self-raising flour
100g castor sugar
100g soft butter or margarine
2 eggs

Method
1. Put 12 cake cases into a tray.
2. Put all the ingredients into a mixing bowl. Beat everything together with a wooden spoon until creamy.
3. Divide the mixture evenly between the cake cases.

Bake for 15–20 minutes

Makes – 12
Oven – Gas 4 or 180°C
Cooking time – 15 to 20 minutes

Shortbread biscuits

This is an easy recipe with only three main ingredients.

You can use biscuit or scone cutters to cut out the shapes or use special biscuit cutters in different shapes, e.g. animals, Christmas shapes.

Ingredients
150g plain flour
50g castor sugar
100g butter or margarine

Method
1. Put the butter or margarine into a bowl. Beat together with a wooden spoon until soft and creamy.
2. Sift the flour into the mixture and stir to make a soft dough.
3. Knead into a ball and roll out.
4. Cut out shapes and place on a greased baking tray (use a palette knife to lift).
5. Bake for 15–20 minutes, until light golden brown.

Oven – Gas 4 or 180°C
Cooking time – 15 to 20 mins

DECORATING CAKES AND BISCUITS

Butter icing is often easier for children to make, and easier to spread on cakes and biscuits than glacé icing – both can be coloured.

With older children you could use ready-made fondant icing. This can be coloured and rolled into different shapes.

Use chocolate buttons, sweets, sugar strands, chocolate vermicelli, cherries, liquorice laces, etc. for decorations.

Butter icing	Glacé icing
Ingredients: 100g butter or margarine 200g icing sugar 1 tsp milk **Method** 1. Put the butter into a bowl and beat until soft. 2. Sift the icing sugar into the softened butter and mix well. 3. Add a little milk to make it creamy.	**Ingredients:** 100g icing sugar Approx 1 tbsp warm water **Method** 1. Sift the icing sugar into a small bowl. 2. Add warm water a little at a time and keep stirring until a thick smooth paste is formed.

Ideas for decorating cakes and biscuits

A child's attempt at decorating cakes

An adult's example of decorated biscuits

OTHER RECIPE IDEAS

Chocolate chip cookies

These are simple to make and don't need much shaping.

Ingredients
75g margarine or butter
75g soft brown sugar
1 egg
150g self-raising flour
100g chocolate chips

Method
1. Put the butter or margarine into a bowl. Beat until soft and creamy.
2. Add the beaten egg, a little at a time, then stir in the flour.
3. Add the chocolate chips.
4. Place spoonfuls of mixture onto a greased baking tray (not too close together).
5. Bake for 10–15 mins.

Makes – depends on size
Oven – Gas 4 or 180°C
Cooking time – 10 to 15 mins

Easy bread

Making and shaping bread is great fun and gives children practice at developing a number of physical skills, especially fine motor skills. It can also be made into interesting shapes such as hedgehogs, snails, tortoises, flowers, letters.

If you make a batch of bread up yourself, it could also be used with younger children who will enjoy being able to handle and shape it.

Ingredients
200g plain flour
½ tsp salt
2 tsp quick acting yeast
1 tablespoon oil
150 ml warm water

Method
1. Put the flour, salt and yeast into a bowl. Add the warm water and oil.
2. Use a wooden spoon to mix to a soft but not sticky dough.
3. Put the dough onto a floured table and knead for 5 mins. Cut into 6–8 even pieces and shape. Place on a baking tray.
4. Put in a warm place until doubled in size.
5. Bake for 10–15 mins.

Makes – 6–8 small rolls or shapes
Oven – Gas 7 or 220°C
Cooking time – 10 to 15 mins

Pizza

Older children could use this recipe to make 4 mini-pizzas. For younger children you could buy ready-made pizza bases and they could help to add the toppings.

Ingredients
1 batch bread dough (as above)
Tomato purée
Selection of toppings e.g. cheese, sliced ham, pieces of sliced pepper, mushrooms, sweetcorn, sliced pepperoni, etc.

Method
1. Make the bread dough (see above). Divide into 4 pieces. Roll each piece out to a circle approx 15 cm across.
2. Spread each circle with 1 tablespoon tomato purée.
3. Decorate the pizzas. Bake for 10 to 15 mins.

OTHER IDEAS FOR FOOD ACTIVITIES

Play dough

Make into food shapes, bake and paint. Use in imaginative play, e.g. parties, cafes and restaurants, shops.

Shopping

Take the child on a shopping trip to the supermarket and let them help to choose simple items. Collect food packaging and set up a shop/supermarket – pretend play.

Eating plates

Collect coloured pictures of different foods from magazines. Stick onto paper plates to make healthy/unhealthy meals. Will help fine motor skills and knowledge of healthy eating.

Make a food book

Use cut-out pictures from magazines or clip-art on a computer to make a book about foods for a child.

Eating out

Take the child to a café or restaurant. Will help social and emotional development as well as fine motor skills.

BOOKS AND STORIES

Books are probably one of the most important 'toys' a child will ever have. Children are never too young to 'read' a book; there are lots of different types and kinds of books to suit all ages and they can be read anytime, anywhere, and they can be enjoyed over and over again.

Long before children can actually 'read' they are learning how books are used – that pages are turned over from right to left, that words usually go across a page from left to right and that pages are usually read from top to bottom.

There are two ways books could be used in your child study visits:

1. You or the child could choose a book or books to read.

2. You could make a book. This could either be *for* the child or *with* the child.

PLANNING AND ORGANISING – READING A BOOK

Although most children enjoy reading books, you need to plan this activity just as carefully as any other. If it is a sunny day, they might not want to sit indoors quietly reading!

 Think About

- The age and stage of development of the child.
- The length of the book – young children cannot concentrate for a long time.
- The language used – this should be suitable for the age of the child.
- The sort of pictures used – these can help the child to follow and understand the story.
- What it is about – think about what the child might enjoy. Younger children need simple stories.
- Stories with rhymes and actions – children can then join in.
- Using different voices and facial expressions when reading.
- Using toys to 'act out' stories.
- Choosing a comfortable quiet area to read with them – away from the TV.
- Going to the library and letting the child choose new books.
- Drawing pictures about the story or characters.

HOW BOOKS AND STORIES CAN HELP DEVELOPMENT

Physical
- Turning pages, following the words with fingers and pointing to pictures all help fine motor skills and hand–eye co-ordination.
- Looking at books and handling them helps sensory development (touch and sight).
- Sense of touch is developed when using books with different textures.
- Sitting still requires physical control.

Social
- Helps children to bond with parents.
- Children get to spend quality individual time with people.
- Books can help children begin to know what is right and wrong.
- Reading can encourage sharing and taking turns.

Emotional
- Provides enjoyment and pleasure.
- Being able to read gives children confidence.
- Being able to read makes children more independent.
- Reading with parents makes children feel loved and secure.
- Children can begin to understand their own feelings through characters in stories.

Intellectual – concepts
- Encourages imagination and creativity.
- Helps to develop memory skills.
- Helps children learn to concentrate.
- Will help to develop an understanding of different concepts, e.g. numbers, letters, colours, size, shape, time, etc.
- Increases knowledge and understanding of their own world and wider world.

Intellectual – language
- Learn new words.
- Encourage children to ask questions.
- Improve listening skills.

Other areas
- Books can help children to learn about and understand a huge range of subjects.
- Develop an awareness of being able to use books as reference and research material.

MAKING A BOOK FOR OR WITH A CHILD

Before planning and making a book, either for or with a child, think about *why* you are doing it and *what* you hope the child will learn from it. This will help you to write your **aims and expectations**.

For example, you might want to use the book to test what the child knows or to help learn something new or be able to understand something better, e.g. numbers, letters, shapes, colours, counting; or you might want it to be more of a creative activity, involving cutting and sticking, painting, drawing and colouring in.

 **Think About**

- ✎ The age, stage of development and skills of the child.
- ✎ What they are interested in.
- ✎ Using simple shapes.
- ✎ Using bright colours.
- ✎ Where you will make it.
- ✎ What materials you will need.
- ✎ How long it will take.
- ✎ Any safety measures you will need to take.

 ## Remember:

You don't have to be brilliant at drawing. You could always use pictures out of magazines, old birthday or Christmas cards, wrapping paper, photographs or even pictures from a computer.

PLANNING AND ORGANISING

You could buy a cheap scrap book or make your own book from paper or thin card punched and held together with string or wool. A5 or A4 size is probably best. Sugar paper is also useful because it can be bought in different colours, is cheap and quite thick so easier to handle.

Depending on what sort of book you are making you will need glue (see glue and sticking, page 77). You will need pencils, crayons, felt tips, pictures, photographs, small pieces of fabric, tissue paper, etc.

You could also put each page into a plastic wallet to make it stronger and easy to wipe clean.

Make a colouring book.

Make a join-the-dots book.

Make a scrap book about your child. Put in pictures of the child, family, any pets, favourite toys, colours, nursery rhymes, songs and so on.

Make an alphabet scrap book with pictures of objects beginning with each letter of the alphabet.

Some ideas for books

Make an activity book.

Make a 'how many' book to help the child recognise shapes and learn to count.

Make a book using pictures from old birthday or Christmas cards.

Make a zig-zag book, which can be hung down or will stand up. Fold a long strip of paper like a concertina. Either put different drawings on each page, e.g. animals, letters, numbers, everyday objects or one simple object like a flower which 'grows' when opened out.

Make up a simple story using your child as the main character – the child could make up the story and you could write it down.

LETTERS, WORDS AND NUMBERS

Activities and games that use letters and words are important because they are the first steps in starting to read and write. In the same way activities and games can help children to begin to understand the concept of numbers and counting, both of which are important in developing maths skills as they get older.

Learning to recognise letters, words and numbers takes a long time and is mainly done through repetition. Making up games and activities using letters, numbers and words can make this more exciting.

 Remember:

Most children will not be able to read, write or do 'sums' until they are 4 or 5.

IDEAS FOR LEARNING LETTERS AND WORDS

Reading stories and looking at books are both important in helping children to begin to recognise letters and simple words. Action rhymes and songs can also help, as can putting labels onto objects around the home.

Word and picture snap
Cut some cards – approx 10 cm × 6 cm. Choose simple words, e.g. ball, cup, sun and write each on several cards. Include picture cards as well. Play snap.

Matching words and pictures
Make up word and picture cards as for the snap cards. Place the cards face up. Match the words. Match the pictures. Match the word to the picture.

Word and picture dominoes
Cut some domino shapes approximately 15 cm × 6 cm. Put letters or simple words and pictures onto the cards.
Spread them out on the floor or on a table, and get the child to try to match them up.

Letter frieze
Draw big outlines of letters onto pieces of card or paper. Let the child colour them in. Join the letters together with string or wool to make the child's name.

Alphabet book
Write each letter of the alphabet at the top of a sheet of paper. Draw or stick pictures of objects beginning with that letter onto the page.

Picture match
Divide a piece of A4 or A3 paper or card into rectangles. Draw simple pictures onto the rectangles. Make up some cards with words or letters to match the picture. Take turns at matching the word cards to the picture.

IDEAS FOR LEARNING NUMBERS

Shops
Make some cardboard coins of 1p, 2p, 5p, 10p. Label the child's toys or books with different prices.

Number cards
Cut 12 card shapes approx 10 cm × 6 cm. On 6 of the cards write the numbers 1–6 and colour in. On the other six draw large spots to match each of the number cards and colour in. Get the child to try to put each of the cards in sequence.
Or match the number cards to the spotted cards. Or take out one of the cards and see which one is missing.

Child's toys labelled with prices

Dot-to-dot book
Make some simple drawings of objects for your child to complete and colour in. By following the numbers on the dot-to-dot objects your child will learn the sequence of counting.

Number wall frieze
Make a decorated wall frieze with your child. Write the numbers 1–10 onto separate sheets of paper or card. Draw simple pictures to match the numbers and colour them in.

 # GAMES

There are lots of games that can be played with or by children, ranging from active games, such as football and hide-and-seek, to pretend/imaginative games where children make up the rules themselves, to board and card games, such as Snap or Lotto.

All are important in different ways in helping different areas of development. Many board and card games are competitive – sometimes these can cause arguments and tantrums and can lessen children's confidence and self-esteem if they lose. Most of these games have rules which have to be followed. They are important because they help children to learn how to:

- share;
- take turns;
- play fairly;
- follow rules.

They also begin to teach children that they may not always win.

> **! ■** 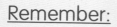 Remember:
>
> When planning to play board games and card games:
> - children under 3 years old will not be able to sit still or concentrate for a long time;
> - children under 3 years old do not understand the idea of rules.

HOW SOME GAMES CAN HELP DEVELOPMENT

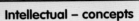

Physical
- 'Simon says' can help develop gross motor skills and balance and co-ordination.
- Games such as snakes and ladders, Connect 4 or Lotto help fine motor skills and hand–eye co-ordination.

Social
- Learning to share.
- Learning to take turns.
- Co-operating with others.

Emotional
- Learn to accept losing.
- May increase self-esteem and confidence.
- May decrease self-esteem and confidence.
- Will experience a variety of both positive and negative emotions.

Other areas
Numeracy
- Board and card games can develop maths concepts and use of mathematical language.

Intellectual – concepts
- Card games and matching games help memory skills and quick thinking.
- Matching games encourage children to recognise how things are similar and different.
- Many games help logical thinking.
- Dice games can help counting and number skills.
- Most games improve concentration.

Intellectual – language
- Encourages communication with others.
- Can increase vocabulary.

 ## MUSIC AND MOVEMENT

Children love to hear music, and from a very early age they respond to musical toys, often with sound and movement. As the child develops they are able to concentrate for longer and so listen to music for longer. From this they can develop their creative and physical skills.

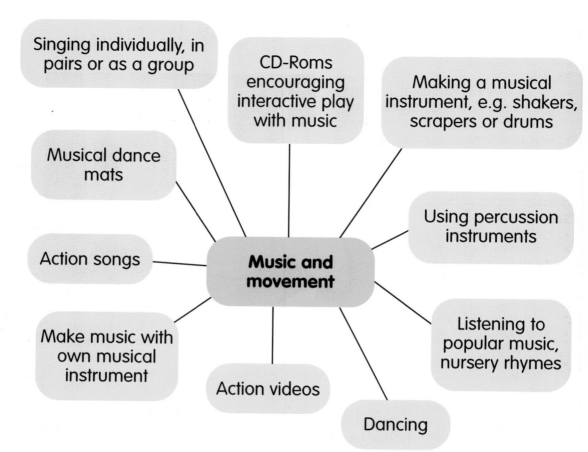

Singing individually, in pairs or as a group

CD-Roms encouraging interactive play with music

Making a musical instrument, e.g. shakers, scrapers or drums

Musical dance mats

Using percussion instruments

Action songs

Music and movement

Make music with own musical instrument

Listening to popular music, nursery rhymes

Action videos

Dancing

PLANNING AND ORGANISING

Plan the activity carefully, ensure you have all the resources before you start.

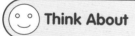 **Think About**

The activities you choose must be:
- suitable for the age of the child you are studying;
- not too easy or too difficult;
- able to keep the child interested.

Once you have chosen what to do, think about:
- materials needed;
- where to set up the activity;
- protecting the area if making an instrument;
- safety.

HOW MUSIC AND MOVEMENT CAN HELP LEARNING AND DEVELOPMENT

Once you have decided on some appropriate activities, think about how they might help you to observe a child's learning and development or how they might link with your research.

Physical
Action songs and dance develop:
- gross motor skills;
- balance;
- co-ordination;
- spatial awareness.

Using keyboards and instruments develops:
- fine motor skills;
- hand–eye co-ordination.

Music and movement develop the senses especially:
- hearing;
- touch.

Music and movement improve:
- breathing;
- muscle tone.
- singing and speaking rhythmically exercises the vocal chords.

Social
When working together with other children music and dance can encourage:
- taking turns;
- sharing;
- consideration for others.

Music and movement from other countries and cultures can help develop understanding and respect for others.

Other areas
- Equal opportunities – knowing about music and instruments from other cultures.
- Vibrating instruments can assist with the development of children with hearing difficulties.
- Music can help to calm children with special needs who respond well to it.

Intellectual – concepts
Music and movement help to develop:
- creativity through moving to different sounds and rhythms;
- the imagination;
- memory and concentration skills;
- listening skills.

Making music can encourage children to:
- explore and experiment;
- develop numeracy skills.

Intellectual – language
- Improves and increases vocabulary.
- Develops knowledge of comparative language.
- Develops non-verbal communication.
- Develops voice tone, range and delivery.
- Encourages communication through facial expression and body movement.

Emotional
Music and movement encourage children to:
- express and share emotions, thoughts and feelings;
- relax;
- increase confidence and self-esteem.

PRACTICAL ACTIVITIES FOR MUSIC, SOUND AND MOVEMENT

Singing and clapping
Any game or song which involves clapping to a rhythm involves listening, repeating and recall.

Repetition
Copying and repeating the tune of a song, even if it is very simple, encourages listening skills and concentration.

Toddler singing and clapping

Mirroring
A child can copy an adult's actions. So stand up and let the child face you. For the child this will be like looking into a mirror.

First you do the actions to music and let the child copy.

Secondly, you could ask the child to do their own actions and you can copy them.

Dancing to music

MAKING MUSICAL INSTRUMENTS

Musical instruments can be made from lots of household objects. Children under the age of five like to play with percussion instruments and they cost very little to make.

Drum

The following household containers make good drums:

- tins empty and clean;
- cake tins;
- saucepans;
- plastic bowls;
- margarine tubs.

Drumsticks

- Wooden spoons, metal spoons and pastry brushes all make great sounds.

Drumstick heads can be made by adding sponge, paper etc.

Shakers

To make shakers you will need a container, such as: plastic bottle with screw top, tin with lid, e.g. cocoa tin, small box.

The best materials to fill the containers are dried pulses, e.g. peas, beans, rice, dried pasta, buttons, milk bottle tops and beads. Put a lid onto the container and seal with tape.

To make a maraca, fill an empty lemon juice container with pulses, then place a wooden stick in the opening and seal with tape.

Remember:

Safety

- Making homemade instruments often uses uncooked pulses, e.g. peas or pieces of wood, etc.
- Take care that small children are supervised during the making of the instruments.

Dancing

All children love to dance on their own or together. Using a CD player you could play a selection of different types of music e.g. fast and slow, high pitch and low pitch, loud and soft.

Some children go to formal classes, e.g. ballet, tap, modern dancing. They may like to put on their special shoes and clothes to show you how to do the dances.

Multi-cultural instruments

A selection of multi-cultural instruments from around the world will let the children expand their knowledge and appreciation of music. Some parents may have their own instrument at home that they may let the child use.

Music for the young

Young children listen to music and sound from an early age. As soon as a child can tap a rattle on the side of their cot they begin to enjoy the noises it makes.

Young children love to drum, shake, match colour coded piano keys and play with percussion instruments.

Exercises to music

Children love to be active and especially like doing simple exercises to music, e.g. stretching and bending, arms stretched high in the air, bending forwards or sideways. Children could do star-jumps or bend their knees to the music. This develops a good sense of balance and rhythm.

Paper and music

A child could make a sound by tearing, scrunching or rubbing different types of paper, such as foil and tissue paper. For example,

'This is how we tear it, tear it, tear it . . . This is how we tear it, just like me.'

The child could repeat this song with different pieces of paper.

Source: *Music Express: Foundation Stage* ISBN 0–7136–6582–3.

RHYMES AND SONGS

Singing songs together

Children love to sing together, particularly if they can put actions to the music and words.

Songs start at an early age when children may sing nursery rhymes.

Action songs

Here are some of the action songs that children enjoy joining in with.

The wheels on the bus	Action
The wheels on the bus go round and round, round and round, round and round The wheels on the bus go round and round All day long	Children move their hands in a circle to show the wheel going round
Other verses can be made up to suit the situation. For example:	
The grannies on the bus go knit one, pearl one	Knitting action
The daddies (or mummies) on the bus go chatter, chatter, chatter	Fingers open and shut
The people on the bus go up and down	Jump up and down
The bell on the bus goes dingalingaling	Pretend to ring a bell
The windscreen wipers go swish, swish, swish	Move arms like wipers

The dingle dangle scarecrow	Action
When all the cows were sleeping And the sun had gone to bed	Children laid on floor asleep
Up jumped the scarecrow and this is what he said	Jump up
'I'm a dingle dangle scarecrow with a flippy, floppy hat	Dangle arms and head Bend head
I shake my hands like this and move my feet like that'	Shake hands and shake feet
Activity	
The child could make a scarecrow puppet using split pins for joints. The child could repeat the song with the puppet doing the actions.	

Counting songs

Counting songs teach a child in a fun way to sequence numbers 1, 2, 3, 4, 5 and so on. They can also teach a child to count backwards. Children can use their fingers to do this either on their own or by copying you.

Ten little gentlemen
Ten little gentlemen standing in a row
Bow little gentlemen, bow down low
Walk little gentlemen, right across the floor
And don't forget gentlemen
To please close the door

Then decrease the number
Nine little gentlemen, etc.

Five little ducks
Five little ducks went swimming one day
Over the hills and far away
Mother duck said 'quack, quack, quack'
And four little ducks came swimming right back

Then continue
Four little, etc. . . .
Three little, etc. . . .
Two little, etc. . . .
One little, etc. . . .

Other songs and rhymes

Here are some titles of songs and rhymes that could be used to support numeracy, concepts, etc.

Counting rhymes

Five little peas
Five currant buns
Ten little mice
Five little ducks
Grand old Duke of York
One man went to mow
Five little leaves
Ten little gentlemen

Transport rhymes

Wheels on the bus
Big, red bus
Row, row, row your boat
The big ship sails
London Bridge
Aeroplanes, aeroplanes

Home rhymes

I'm a little teapot
Wind the bobbin up
There was an old woman who lived in a shoe
Hickory, dickory dock
Here is the house
Mix a pancake
Polly put the kettle on
With my little broom

Animal rhymes

Ding dong bell
Pop! goes the weasel
Hey diddle diddle
This little piggy
The garden snail
Mr Giraffe
Old Mcdonald
Swim little fish
Incy wincey spider

Other rhymes

Humpty Dumpty
See-saw Margorie Daw
Here is the church
Pat-a-cake
Rock a bye, baby
Hot cross buns
Oranges and lemons
Tom, Tom, tomato

PHYSICAL OUTDOOR PLAY

Most toys, games and activities will involve some sort of physical movement, and will help, in different ways, to develop physical skills. Many children's toys, games and activities tend to be done indoors and often concentrate on using fine motor skills.

As children grow, and become more mobile and curious, they need the chance to explore and investigate the world they live in, and they usually have lots of energy which most indoor activities will not use up. They need to exercise and develop their larger body muscles in arms and legs by running, jumping, climbing, skipping. To do this they need to have lots of outdoor play, with space to run around and 'let off steam'.

This sort of play is also important because it gives children a chance to meet, play and mix with other children, and people of different ages and cultures, which is an important part of their social development. It encourages sharing, taking turns and learning to co-operate.

Outdoor play is also important because it gives children a chance to explore different environments.

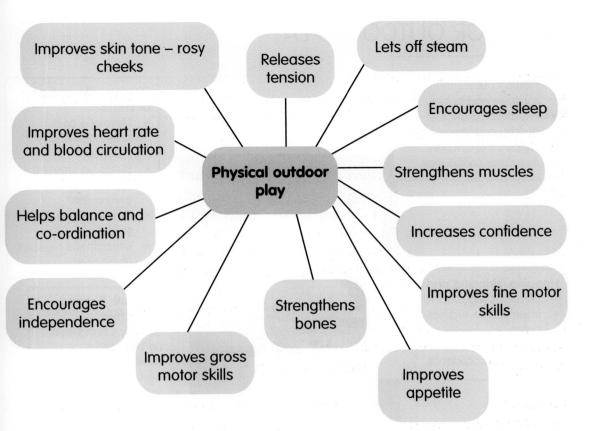

Physical outdoor play

- Improves skin tone – rosy cheeks
- Releases tension
- Lets off steam
- Encourages sleep
- Improves heart rate and blood circulation
- Strengthens muscles
- Helps balance and co-ordination
- Increases confidence
- Encourages independence
- Strengthens bones
- Improves fine motor skills
- Improves gross motor skills
- Improves appetite

PLANNING AND ORGANISING

When planning and organising outdoor activities it is very important to think carefully about safety, as well as how you think it will help the child to learn and develop.

Remember:

At no time should you have sole responsibility for looking after a young child – so ask the parent/s to go with you.

Think About

- Where will you go and how you will get there.
- What facilities are available.
- Checking to see if it is suitable for the age of your child – visit first.
- Carrying out a risk assessment.
- Suitable clothing for the child to wear.

Most importantly
- Get permission from the parents.

IDEAS FOR OUTDOOR PLAY

Riding a bike
- Helps to strengthen leg muscles and bones.
- Improves balance.
- Builds up stamina.
- Helps co-ordination.
- Increases confidence.

Playing hide-and-seek or chase
- Develops co-ordination and balance.
- Builds up stamina.
- Improves spatial awareness.
- Develops social skills.
- Strengthens muscles and bones.

Hopping, skipping and jumping
- Develops leg muscles.
- Improves co-ordination and balance.
- Improves stamina.
- Builds up confidence.

Playing with bat and ball or skittles
- Develops hand–eye co-ordination.
- Develops arm and leg muscles.
- Encourages co-operative play.
- Improves stamina.

Climbing
- Improves balance and co-ordination.
- Develops problem solving.
- Develops arm and leg muscles.
- Increases confidence.

Child learning to ride on a tricycle

Playing with snowballs
- Increases strength in arm and leg muscles.
- Improves co-ordination.
- Encourages imaginative play.

All of these activities will give children the chance to 'let off steam' and fresh air will help them to sleep better and improve their appetite.

OTHER IDEAS FOR OUTDOOR PLAY

- Make stepping stones out of pieces of card and place them around the garden – get the child to walk across the stones.
- Go for a walk in the country or on the beach. Collect interesting objects, e.g. leaves, shells. Use these to make a collage when you get home.
- Create a small garden for the child to look after. Plant some quick growing seeds.
- Take a trip to the beach to build sandcastles.

SAND AND WATER

Playing with sand and water develops many skills. It involves messy play, creative play and uses natural materials. It also encourages children to begin to develop problem solving skills as they experiment with designs and learn through trial and error, e.g. building dams, castles.

PLANNING AND ORGANISING
PLAYING WITH SAND AND WATER

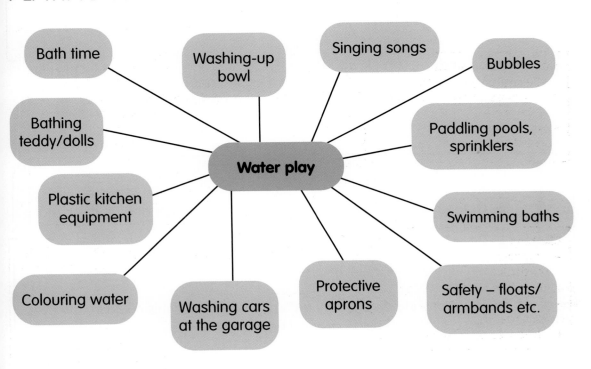

 Remember:

♦ Never leave babies and toddlers alone when playing with water. They could drown in even small amounts of water.
♦ Hot taps could burn delicate skin so cover with flannels.
♦ Sharp objects in or around the bath need to be protected.
♦ Don't allow the child to drink the bath or play water.

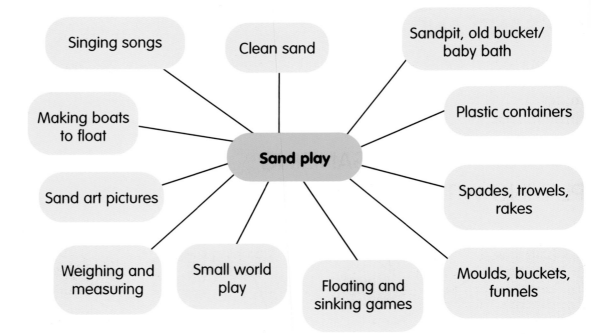

Singing songs

Clean sand

Sandpit, old bucket/ baby bath

Making boats to float

Plastic containers

Sand play

Sand art pictures

Spades, trowels, rakes

Weighing and measuring

Small world play

Floating and sinking games

Moulds, buckets, funnels

Remember:

- ◆ Outdoor sandpits must be covered to prevent cats and other animals getting into the sand.
- ◆ Clean the sand regularly. Do this by rinsing with water containing a steriliser. This could be like the one used for sterilising babies' bottles.
- ◆ Children should be taught not to throw sand as this could irritate eyes. Rinse eyes with cold water if it happens.

Think About

Choose activities carefully. They must be:
- ✎ suitable for the age of the child you are studying;
- ✎ approved by the parent/carer. Will the activity be too messy? This type of activity could only take place with parental support;
- ✎ neither too easy nor too difficult.

Once you have chosen what to do you need to check:
- ✎ equipment needed;
- ✎ hygiene of the equipment;
- ✎ when the activity will take place;
- ✎ safety;
- ✎ allergies the child may have to touching any materials.

> **Remember:**
> You are not expected to be in sole charge of the child.

HOW SAND AND WATER PLAY CAN HELP LEARNING DEVELOPMENT

Physical
- Hand and eye co-ordination pouring water into vessels.
- Control and strengthening of muscles in the hands and arms.
- Fine motor skills with spreading, spooning etc.

Sensory
- Development of touch/texture.

Social
- Sharing space, equipment.
- Understanding personal hygiene rules.

Emotional
- Develops a sense of fun and enjoyment.
- Children gain confidence.

Intellectual – concepts
- Organisational skills, sequence and patterns.
- Learning about natural materials.
- Pouring water/sand into different sized vessels develops the concepts of size, shape, capacity, volume.
- Creative development, using materials imaginatively.
- Understanding rules about safety and danger.
- Problem solving

Intellectual – language
- Extends the vocabulary with new words, e.g. splish, splosh.
- Develops descriptive language.
- Language to negotiate.

PLAYING WITH WATER

Water activities could be played in the bath, in a clean washing-up bowl, a bucket, a paddling pool or the kitchen sink. It could get very messy so check out with an adult first before you start.

TOP TIPS

- Your child should use a waterproof protective apron with sleeves and close-fitting cuffs.
- Bowls of water could be placed on a draining board or outside in the garden.
- A plastic protective sheet could be used on the floor if spills occur.

In the warmer weather children love to play outside in the garden using a paddling pool, hose pipe and sprinkler or even an old baby bath.

Using lots of plastic equipment, e.g. cups, bowls, watering cans and sieves, children can play for hours enjoying the fresh air and developing their skills.

Child outside playing with cups and water

Playing with bubbles is great fun. A variety of simple containers could be used. Straws are good to make bubbles with and there a variety of play products in toy shops to assist with this type of play.

!

Remember:

◆ Take care with water activities.
◆ Do not leave the child unattended.
◆ Hot taps can burn a child.
◆ Children playing outside may require protection from the sun.

PLAYING WITH SAND

Playing with sand does not require a sand pit – an old washing up bowl, tyre, seed tray or any other suitable container would be acceptable. Clean and cheap play sand can be bought from toy shops.

A range of objects can be used when playing with sand, including sand pens, brushes with rubber tips, rolling tubes, paint-effect rollers, buckets and spades, wheels, moulds, shapes, trucks and diggers.

Children playing a game with sand, buckets, spade and a wheelbarrow

> ## Remember:
> Outdoor sand pits should be covered. This is to prevent animals contaminating the sand and to stop water collecting inside which could be dangerous if a toddler fell in.

 ACTIVITIES FOR YOUNG BABIES

Studying a very young baby can be difficult. In their first three months babies tend to sleep most of the time – sometimes 20 out of every 24 hours. They wake up only when they are hungry, cold or uncomfortable.

During this stage, they have very little control over their physical actions – although they can hold things. This is a **reflex action**. They can only focus on objects, such as toys, if they are held close to them (about 25 cm) and babies communicate mainly by crying.

From three months, development begins to speed up and is easier to recognise, and during the rest of their first year their main development will be physical.

This does not mean that you should ignore intellectual, emotional or social development, because it will certainly be happening! However, from the moment they are born, babies learn through their senses – mainly by touching, tasting (mouthing), listening and seeing. So it is very important that they:

- have a lot of close physical contact (being held and cuddled);
- are spoken to when being fed, changed, bathed, held;
- have lots of stimulus to look at when they are not being handled, e.g. mobiles, freezes and pictures on walls;
- have lots of 'play' times with parents and carers.

Babies will also quickly learn to communicate in different ways, different tones of cries will mean different things, and they will begin to gurgle, babble, use jargon, etc. until they begin to speak their first words.

They learn to socialise – mainly with parents and close family – but then gradually begin to accept others.

Although emotional development may seem slow, they will begin to show a range of different feelings – from happiness and contentment to shyness, frustration and anxiety.

Although it might seem easier to plan activities for toddlers and children, it is important to remember that unless babies are given lots of time and attention from parents and carers, and chances to play, they may not develop at an 'average' rate.

PLANNING AND ORGANISING

Think About

Obviously you need to think, choose and plan carefully. It is really important that you:
- know exactly what babies can be expected to do at different stages in the first three months (check in text books);
- think about how you could use their toys to help them develop skills;
- understand that you may not always see a lot of change and progression – and because of this you may have to plan to do similar activities over several visits so that you can notice how they *have* changed or improved.

Above all, remember that babies learn through their senses.

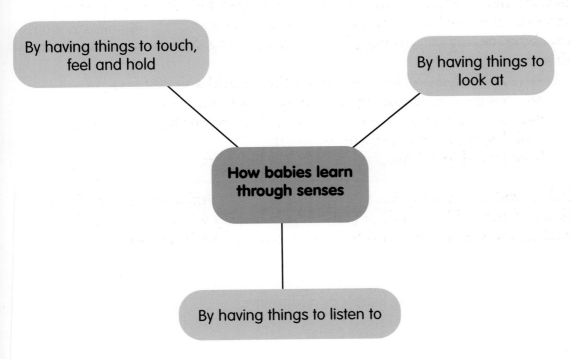

Check out the following milestones for physical and sensory development.

	Gross motor skills	Fine motor skills	Sensory
At birth	• Reflex actions e.g. skipping or walking reflex.	• Reflex actions, e.g. grasp reflex.	• Reflex actions, e.g. startle reflex.
At 1 month	• May begin to lift head when laid on tummy. • Will enjoy kicking.	• Can open and close hands.	• Can see objects close to them (25 cm). • Moves head towards sound.
At 3 months	• Learning to support head. • Kicks vigorously. • Moves head to look at what parents are doing.	• Clasps hands together. • Looks at hands and plays with fingers. • Can hold a toy for a short time.	• Can focus on toys. • May turn in right direction if name is called. • Begins to look around.
At 6 months	• Can sit, if supported by cushions. • Can roll over. • May try to crawl.	• Will pass toys from hand to hand. • Grabs toys using whole hand palmar grasp.	• Puts all objects to mouth. • Becoming alert and curious about what goes on around them.

When planning activities and visits, try to look at what the baby can do now *and* should be able to do next. This should help you to choose activities which will encourage the *next* stage of development.

It can be a good idea to observe babies when they are being fed, in the bath or being changed and played with by their parents.

This can help you to see exactly how they behave and react, and you can then compare this to 'average' milestones. You can also see how parents play with and encourage their baby's development.

Remember:
- Don't be tempted to make these into three separate visits, as you may not have enough to observe.
- Don't be tempted to observe all three at **every** visit. This would make your study very repetitive. To see any real change and progression in what babies can do and how they react, you could repeat this visit after two or three months.

OTHER IDEAS

The following are simple ideas for activities for a very young baby, which could help you look at different areas of development.

Remember:
- Try to do three or four different activities at each visit so you can check different areas of development.
- Look at the baby's reactions carefully and write them down.

Encouraging vision and head movement
Hold a simple, brightly coloured toy or rattle close to face (25 cm). *Slowly* move from side to side. As the baby gets better at this, move toy further from side to side or try moving it up and down, backwards and forwards.

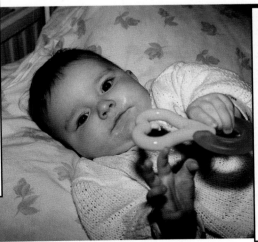

Baby holding a brightly coloured rattle

Encouraging vision, hearing and communication skills
Talk to your baby. Hold the baby carefully, supporting the neck but facing your face. Talk to and smile at the baby – give the baby time to reply. Although they cannot speak, they will concentrate on your movements and begin to gurgle and smile.

Encouraging sight and fine motor skills
Try making a simple mobile to hang above a cot, or a toy which will stretch across the cot for the baby to look at and reach out to.
You could use a covered coat-hanger for the mobile (e.g. tinsel) and strong elastic fastened to each side of the cot. Try to choose things which would show different sounds, textures and shapes.
Some ideas – ribbons, card cut into shapes or faces and decorated, Christmas tree baubles, shapes with different patterns, yogurt pots, foil crumpled into shapes, spirals cut out of card. This will encourage the child to explore the senses.

> ## Remember:
> Check all items are safe.

Encouraging gross motor skills
Once babies begin to get stronger, encourage gross motor skills by putting favourite toys just out of reach – this will encourage them to roll over.

Encouraging sensory development
Once your baby can sit reasonably well, even if supported by cushions, make a feely bag or basket of different items of different textures (not toys), e.g. face cloth; small plastic bottle filled with rice; large pine cone; large, clean, smooth stone; woollen pom pom; clothes peg; hair brush, etc.

Older baby reaching out exploring a new texture

- ◆ Compare what you see to what textbooks say about development.
- ◆ Try the same activities at a later visit – perhaps after two months – to see how the baby has improved.

> ## Remember:
>
> **Testing reflexes – new baby**
> Check what reflex actions a new baby will have.
> Ask the parents if they will help you to test these. DO NOT TEST THESE YOURSELF – new babies need very careful handling.
> Check again after 1 month.

OTHER WAYS TO ENCOURAGE DEVELOPMENT

 Sing simple songs and action rhymes to your baby, e.g. 'Pat-a-cake', 'Round and round the garden', 'This little piggy', etc.

Once baby can hold a toy, give them something to bang on, e.g. wooden spoon on pans, cake tins, etc.

Try passing toys between you and the baby as you talk to them. This will encourage fine motor skills and taking turns.

And, of course, do not forget to use your baby's own toys. Look at what is played with, how and for how long.

Development of the child

In this section you will find information on all four areas of development (physical, intellectual, emotional and social) plus ideas for toys and play activities. It is organised according to age. This will be useful when planning visits and activities.

➡ DEVELOPMENTAL MILESTONES

The age and stage at which children grow and develop depends on many factors. When studying children's development we usually refer to developmental **milestones**. These are stages at which a child masters a skill, and are usually linked to a specific age. In this section we are going to look at the major physical, intellectual, emotional and social milestones.

It is important to remember that these milestones are only a *guide* – all children are different and individual and will develop at different rates.

NEWBORN BABIES

At birth all babies are totally dependent on their parents, but from the moment they are born they begin to learn and explore the world around them. They do this through their senses.

Although they can only focus on objects held close to them (25 cm) when awake they will look around, watch and, when held, will focus intently on the face of the person holding them.

They quickly begin to recognise their main carer by the sound of his or her voice and through their own sense of smell.

They communicate by crying – but they soon cry in different ways for different reasons, e.g. hunger, boredom, tiredness.

At first they have no voluntary control over their body. They cannot move from back to front. When lying on their backs their head is usually on one side, and when on their stomachs they will lie with their knees tucked up, bottoms in the air and their head to one side.

Their hands are usually tightly closed.

Newborn babies do have a number of movements called **reflexes**. These are involuntary movements (ones which they cannot control) which are inborn and made automatically, and are important in helping the baby to survive. Most of these reflexes disappear by about 3 months.

The swallowing and sucking reflex

If a finger is placed in a baby's mouth they will automatically suck and swallow – this helps them feed. Sometimes babies are born with sore fingers because they have sucked them in the womb.

The rooting reflex

If a finger is gently stroked across the baby's cheek, they will automatically turn their heads towards it, as it searches for a nipple or teat.

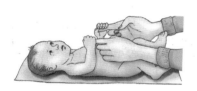

The grasping reflex

If an object or finger is placed in the palm of their hand, babies will automatically grasp it tightly.

The walking reflex

If babies are held in a standing position, with the soles of their feet touching the floor, they will make stepping movements as if trying to walk.

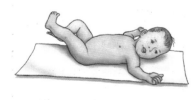

The startle reflex

If startled by a sudden bright light or a noise babies will close their hand into a fist, bend their elbows and bring their arms towards their shoulders. They may also cry.

The falling reflex (Moro reflex)

Any sudden movement affecting the neck makes babies think they may be dropped. This makes them throw their arms back, then bring them together as though they were trying to catch a ball.

THREE MONTHS

Babies are still completely dependent on other people. They are beginning to show more interest in their surroundings. Reflex actions are disappearing and fine and gross motor skills are beginning to develop. They may begin to play with simple toys, such as a rattle, and communicate with smiles and gurgles.

Physical
Gross motor skills
- When lying on front can lift head and turn from side to side.
- When lying on front, can push up on arms and raise shoulders.
- Can kick legs strongly.
- If held in a sitting position, head will lag very little.
- When held can sit with a straight back.

Fine motor skills
- Can hold a small toy for a short time.
- Looks at their hands and plays with hands and fingers.
- Grasp reflex may have disappeared.

Sensory
- Finds hands and brings them to mouth.
- Begins to move head to look at things when hearing a voice.
- Will turn towards the sound.
- Fascinated by faces.

Intellectual – concepts
- Becoming more aware of surroundings.
- Begins to use mouth to explore objects.
- May smile when spoken to by carer.
- Looks intently at things which move.

Intellectual – language
- Coos and gurgles to show contentment.
- May smile when spoken to by carer.
- May begin to babble.
- Beginning to control muscles of lips, tongue, voice box.

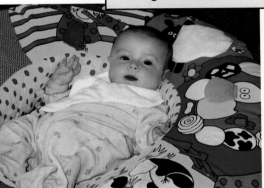

Social
- Smiles at both family and strangers.
- Enjoys time with carers, e.g. bath time and feeding.

Emotional
- Becomes very attached to mother or main carer.
- Shows feelings and emotions.
- Shows pleasure when held.

Toys and activities

Mobiles above or attached to cot. Soft toys and balls. Rattles, teething rings and other hand-held toys which are safe to put into mouth. Young babies should be held close, talked or sung to often.

SIX MONTHS

By six months babies can usually sit on their own for some time without support. They are becoming more interested and curious, and will explore everything they pick up by 'mouthing'. They enjoy being with people and being played with but are becoming unsure of strangers.

Physical
Gross motor skills
- Can lift head and chest clear of floor supported by arms.
- Can sit for long periods if supported by cushions.
- Can sit for short periods without support but will 'topple' over.
- May try to roll over from back to front.
- May try to crawl.
- When lying on back, grasps legs and feet and puts feet into the mouth.
- Kicks strongly when lying on back.
- May hold out hands to be picked up.

Fine motor skills
- Puts all objects to mouth (**mouthing**).
- Grabs toys using whole hand (**palmar grasp**).
- Will pass toys from hand to hand.
- Begins to reach out for small toys.
- Can pass toys from one hand to the other.
- Has learnt to drop things.

Sensory
- Still 'mouths' toys and objects.
- Looks around curiously.
- If a toy falls out of sight will not look for it.
- Watches what people are doing.

Intellectual – concepts
- Knows to hold out arms to be picked up.
- Can recognise mother's or main carer's voice and will turn towards them.
- Spatial awareness is improving so may notice toys that are half hidden.

Intellectual – language
- Cooing may cease.
- Babbling is more repetitive, e.g. da da da, and more tuneful (**echolalia**).
- Laughs, chuckles and squeals.
- Screams with annoyance.
- May understand simple words, e.g. bye bye, mama.
- Begins to imitate – repeat sounds.

Social
- Enjoys being played with.
- May display **separation anxiety**.
- May be afraid of strangers.
- May feed using fingers.
- May begin to play with family members in a simple way, e.g. stroking face.
- May play alone (**solitary play**) with a simple toy, e.g. rattle.

Emotional
- Will enjoy being played with.
- Laughs with pleasure.
- May 'cling' to mother or main carer for security.

Toys and play

As for 3 months, plus activity centres, non-breakable mirrors, activity mats with textures and hidden noises, bath toys, cardboard boxes to put toys in, simple picture books, things to bang, playing 'Peek-a-boo' and 'This little piggy'.

NINE MONTHS

Baby is now becoming more mobile and will be beginning to crawl or 'cruise'. Can now sit for long periods of time and reach for things without toppling over. Language skills are beginning to develop. They are usually shy with strangers.

Physical
Gross motor skills
- Tries to crawl by rocking backwards and forwards.
- Can pull into a standing position by going onto knees first.
- May begin to sidestep – **cruise** – around furniture.
- May begin to crawl upstairs.
- Can sit unsupported for longer periods of time.
- When sitting, can turn to look sideways and stretch to reach toys.
- May take some steps if held.

Fine motor skills
- Uses **primitive pincer grasp** (thumb and first finger) to pick up small objects.
- Cannot voluntarily 'let go' of toys.
- Will begin to look for dropped or hidden objects which are out of sight.
- Uses index finger to point.

Sensory
- Looks in correct place for fallen toys.
- Begins to recognise familiar pictures.
- Enjoys joining in games such as 'Peek-a-boo'.

Intellectual – concepts
- Can tell the difference between family and strangers.
- Recognises familiar games and rhymes.
- Recognises own name and will turn head when spoken to.
- Has no concept of danger.
- May look for a toy they see being hidden (**object permanence**).

Intellectual – language
- Repeats syllables, e.g. dad dad, mum mum, ba ba.
- Uses sound deliberately to express emotions.
- Imitates sounds, e.g. blows raspberries, smacks lips.
- May understand simple words, e.g. no, bye bye.

Social
- May drink from a cup without help.
- Will still need to be close to a familiar adult.
- Will be happy to play alone.
- May hold out hands to be washed.

Emotional
- May need a comfort object or toy to take to bed, e.g. teddy.
- May still show fear of strangers.

Toys and play

As for 6 months, plus rattles and toys which will stick to surfaces, balls of different sizes and textures, stacking toys, fabric, card or plastic books, large soft bricks, feely bags or boxes. Will enjoy songs and rhymes with actions, e.g. 'Pat-a-cake'.

TWELVE MONTHS

By 12 months the world is becoming a bigger and more interesting place because children are now becoming more mobile as they learn to crawl and walk. Also at around this age language development starts to 'take off'. Socially and emotionally, children will still be shy with others and need to be close to parents/carers.

Physical
Gross motor skills
- Becoming very mobile – either by crawling, shuffling, bear walking or bottom shuffling.
- Can walk a few steps if held.
- May start to walk but will tend to fall or sit suddenly.
- Can sit unsupported for long periods of time.
- Tries to crawl upstairs forwards and downstairs backwards.
- Can stand alone.

Fine motor skills
- Uses a neat **pincer grasp** (thumb and first finger) to pick up small objects.
- Points to objects with index finger.
- Uses both hands, but may begin to show preference for one.
- Puts small objects into a container, e.g. bricks into a beaker.
- Drops and throws toys deliberately.
- Uses **tripod grasp** to hold bricks and bang them together.
- May hold a crayon in a **palmar grasp**.
- May try to turn pages in a book but usually several at once.

Sensory
- Watches people, animals and moving objects for long periods.
- Drops and watches falling toys.
- Looks for lost or hidden toys.
- Recognises familiar people and sounds.
- Turns to sound.

Intellectual – concepts
- Is learning through trial and error.
- Will pick up toys and hand them to others, when asked.
- Can understand and act on simple instructions, e.g. wave bye bye.

Intellectual – language
- Imitates simple words.
- Recognises simple words and points, showing **understanding**.
- Babbling becomes more tuneful and similar to speech.
- Learns first words (**active vocabulary**).
- Understands more words than they can vocalise (**passive vocabulary**).
- Talks incessantly in their own language (**jargon**).

Social
- Will still want to be close to familiar people.
- Enjoy others' company, especially at meal times.
- Use fingers to feed themselves.
- May drink from a feeding cup by themselves.
- May help dressing by holding out leg/arm.

Emotional
- Shows affection for parents and family.
- Needs to hold hands to feel secure.

Toys and play

As for 9 months, plus musical toys and boxes, simple jigsaws, bricks and containers, push and pull toys, picture books with simple rhymes, 'hide-and-seek' games. Will also enjoy sand and water play, play dough and copying adults, e.g. dusting.

FIFTEEN MONTHS

> By 15 months children are much more mobile and can walk along but may bump into furniture. Fine motor skills are developing well and they may enjoy simple drawing activities. They are still very egocentric and learn through trial and error.

Physical
Gross motor skills
- Walks independently using arms to balance.
- Can crawl downstairs, feet first.
- Throws a large ball but may fall over.
- Can kneel without support.
- Can get up to a standing position without using the help of people or furniture.

Fine motor skills
- Claps hands together.
- Can build a tower of two blocks.
- Can pick up and drink from a cup using two hands to hold it.
- Make a mark with a crayon using a **palmar grasp**.
- Turns pages in a book but will turn several at once.
- Tries to eat with a spoon but will turn it upside down.

Sensory
- Looks with interest at pictures in a book and pats them.
- Stands at a window and watches what is happening for long periods of time.

Intellectual – concepts
- Understands **object permanence** – things exist even if they cannot be seen.
- Still very **egocentric**.
- More adventurous and wants to explore.
- Grasps crayon half way up with **palmar grasp** with either hand.
- Scribbles to and fro.

Intellectual – language
- Uses several words which parents can understand.
- Points and uses single words to indicate an item.
- Beginning to use words to communicate.

Emotional
- Shows love and affection to family members.

Social
- Becoming more helpful – will try to dress themselves but will need help.
- Can hold a cup and drink from it without help.
- May begin to understand when they want to go to the toilet but cannot control muscles.
- Still shy with strangers.

Toys and play

As for 12 months, plus soft balls to throw, building bricks, cause and effect toys, e.g. Jack-in-the-box, drawing and simple gluing activities, listening to nursery rhymes and stories, dancing to music.

EIGHTEEN MONTHS

> By this age children can walk well, are becoming more adventurous and want to explore but have little understanding of danger. Fine motor skills are much improved and language skills are beginning to develop fast. They are becoming more sociable.

Physical
Gross motor skills
- Can walk confidently and steadily without using arms to balance.
- Can pick up toys by bending from waist.
- Can 'squat' to look for things without losing balance.
- May be able to walk up and down stairs without adult help.
- Runs, but sometimes bumps into obstacles.
- Can push and pull toys when walking.
- Can crawl backwards downstairs.

Fine motor skills
- Can turn knobs and handles on doors.
- Can build a tower of three bricks.
- Can string together four large beads.
- Uses **mature pincer grasp**.
- Beginning to use the **tripod grasp** when using pencils and crayons.
- Can pull off shoes.
- Fascinated by buttons, zips, other fastenings.

Sensory
Hand–eye co-ordination is good – can:
- pick up small objects such as beads with **delicate pincer grasp**;
- enjoys simple picture books;
- recognises and points to brightly coloured items on a page;
- recognises familiar people at a distance.

Intellectual – concepts
- Can recognise and point to pictures in a book if asked.
- Memory is developing.
- When drawing uses scribbles and dots.
- Tries to imitate adult actions.
- Starts to match shapes to holes in a shape sorter.
- Knows and can point to parts of the body.
- Recognises objects from books and pictures.
- May start to do simple jigsaws.

Intellectual – language
- Active vocabulary increases.
- Words are used to mean more than one thing, e.g. 'cup' may mean 'where is my cup?', 'I want my cup', 'I've dropped my cup'.
- Echoes and repeats words (**echolalia**).
- Enjoys trying to copy rhymes and simple songs.
- Words are symbolic, e.g. dog is used for any four legged animal (**holophrases**).

Emotional
- Will show different and strong emotions – e.g. fear, anger, happiness.
- May change from negative to positive emotions quickly.
- Becoming more independent.

Social
- Becoming more sociable.
- May refuse to obey instructions.
- Still **egocentric** and shy of strangers, needing a familiar adult close to them.
- Play happily alone (**solitary play**).
- May enjoy playing alongside others (**parallel play**).
- Can use a cup and spoon well.
- Can take off clothing quite easily and help to dress themselves.
- Can give warning that they need the toilet by words and actions.

Toys and play

As for 15 months, plus shape sorters, hammering toys, toy telephones, play dough, musical toys, books with joining-in activities, simple story books. Will enjoy simple sticking and gluing, modelling and finger painting, circle games, e.g. 'Ring-a-ring-a-roses' and songs and rhymes with actions.

TWO YEARS

At this age children can run, walk and talk and are becoming more independent. They are curious and want to explore but still have only limited understanding of danger. When frustrated or stopped from doing something they throw temper tantrums. Pretend play is important at this stage.

Physical
Gross motor skills
- Can walk up and down stairs confidently two feet to a step.
- Enjoys climbing on furniture.
- Can kick a large ball that is not moving.
- Enjoys toys which are put together and pulled apart.
- Walks and runs more safely and steadily.
- Pushes and pulls large wheeled toys.
- Can sit on a tricycle and use feet to move it.

Fine motor skills
- Can turn pages of a book one by one.
- Has good hand–eye co-ordination.
- Can build a tower of 5 or 6 bricks.
- Uses **mature pincer grasp** to pick up and position small objects.
- Holds a pencil firmly and can form circles, lines and dots.
- Can zip and unzip large zippers.
- Uses preferred hand.

Sensory
- Enjoys looking at picture books.
- Recognises fine detail in favourite pictures.
- Recognises familiar adults in photographs.

Intellectual – concepts
- May make a letter V when drawing.
- Vertical lines and circular scribble forming.
- May begin to sort and match.
- Uses **symbolic play**, e.g. a twig from a tree will become a sword.
- Still very **egocentric**.
- Enjoys books.
- Learns by copying and imitating adults.

Intellectual – language
- Is learning new words quickly.
- Has a larger vocabulary.
- May use **telegraphic sentences**, e.g. me want ball.
- Beginning to use pronouns, e.g. me, I, you.
- Beginning to ask questions.
- Talks non-stop.
- Begins to use negatives, e.g. no teddy.

Emotional
- Will act out feelings and ideas through **pretend play**.
- Will have tantrums and show strong emotions when frustrated.
- Becoming more independent but will still often cling to an adult.
- May still display **separation anxiety**.

Social
- Will play near other children (**parallel play**).
- Still finds it hard to share.
- Can feed without too much mess and uses a spoon well.
- Can lift a cup and put it down without spilling.
- By 2½ may be able to pour a drink for themselves.
- Can put on some clothing themselves.
- By 2½ can unfasten buttons, zips and buckles.
- Can say when they need the toilet.
- By 2½ should be dry during the day – may be dry at night.

Toys and play

As for 18 months, plus dressing-up clothes, construction toys, dolls and teddies for pretend play, musical toys, e.g. xylophone. Outdoor toys could include simple climbing frame, small slides and swings, sit and ride toys, paddling pools. May enjoy painting and colouring-in and simple printing.

THREE YEARS

By this age children are much more independent and confident. They become less frustrated when trying to do things because they are becoming more skilful, so temper tantrums are less frequent. They are trusting, and more sociable, so will play with others and enjoy creative and pretend play.

Physical
Gross motor skills
- Can walk and run forwards with precision.
- Can walk on tip toe.
- Can kick a ball forwards.
- Can throw overhand.
- Can catch a large ball with extended arms.
- Pedals and steers a tricycle.
- Walks upstairs with one foot on each step.
- Can hop on one foot.
- Can manoeuvre around objects showing **spatial awareness**.

Fine motor skills
- Holds a crayon with more control and can draw a face.
- Can eat with a spoon and fork without spilling.
- Can colour in more neatly and more within lines.
- Can put on and take off coat.
- Can build a tower of 9 or 10 bricks.
- Cuts with toy scissors.
- Uses **improved tripod grasp**.

Sensory
- Knows name of some colours.
- Can match 2 or 3 primary colours, usually red and yellow.
- Listens eagerly to favourite stories and wants to hear them over and over again.
- Can thread large beads.

Intellectual – concepts
- Beginning to understand concept of time – especially past and future.
- Beginning to understand number concept of 1 and lots.
- Beginning to use language to describe thoughts and ideas
- Can count up to 10 by rote.
- Enjoys music, both making it and listening to it.
- Concentrates for longer periods of time.
- Understands concepts of **cause and effect**.
- Enjoys **pretend play**.
- Can copy a circle but does not always join it up.
- May write letters V, H and T.
- Draws a head with one or two features.

Intellectual – language
- Vocabulary is large.
- Sentences are longer and close to adult speech.
- Often holds long, imaginary conversations when playing.
- Incessantly asks questions: why, when, where, what.
- May use incorrect word endings, e.g. drawed, sheeps.

Emotional
- Shows feelings and concern for others.
- Sometimes develops fears, e.g. dark.
- Temper tantrums are not as frequent.
- May have outgrown **separation anxiety**.

Social
- Can use a fork and spoon to eat.
- Will go the toilet on their own during day.
- Should be dry at night.
- Can wash their hands but not dry them properly.
- Becoming independent – wanting to dress themselves.
- Will begin to show interest in other children and to play with them (**joining-in play**).
- More trusting.

Toys and play

As for 2 years, plus small world toys, pop-up books or books with lift-up flaps. Simple cooking, drawing and painting, building things. Will enjoy making 'dens', helping in the house, matching and sorting games, riding tricycle.

FOUR YEARS

By this age gross and fine motor skills are quite well developed. Children are creative and imaginative, and enjoy making things. Language skills are good – they enjoy playing with other children and can usually take turns and may begin to understand rules. They are curious and love to explore and investigate.

Physical
Gross motor skills
- Can walk or run alone, and walk up and down stairs, in adult fashion.
- Can walk along a straight line.
- Climbs ladders and trees.
- Pedals and controls a tricycle confidently.
- Is becoming more skilled at ball games – can throw, catch, bounce and kick a ball and use a bat.

Fine motor skills
- Can build a tower of 10 or more blocks.
- Can build 3 steps with 6 bricks, if shown how.
- Uses a **mature pincer grasp**.
- Can fasten and unfasten buttons.
- Can put together large piece jigsaws.
- Can colour in pictures, but not always within the lines.

Sensory
- Matches and names 4 primary colours.
- Follows story books with eyes and identifies words and pictures.

Intellectual – concepts
- Can count up to 10 by rote.
- Beginning to understand number concept 1–3.
- Understands concept of past and future.
- Still muddles fact with fiction.
- Enjoys jokes.
- Can repeat songs and rhymes without mistakes.
- May know letters of the alphabet.
- Beginning to understand concept of right and wrong.
- Can concentrate for longer periods.
- May be able to copy letters V, H, T and O.
- Begins to trace shapes, letters and numbers formed by dots.
- Draws a potato person with head, legs, trunk.
- May not have fingers or toes on arms or legs.

Intellectual – language
- May use about 1,500 words.
- Talks about past and future.
- Sentences are more grammatically correct but may still get endings wrong.
- Uses a variety of questions.
- Uses positional words e.g. in, over, under.
- May mispronounce words.
- May mix up sounds like 'th' or 'f'.

Emotional
- Will be very affectionate towards family friends and people they see often.
- More trusting.
- Will tell their thoughts and feelings to people.
- Shows love for younger brothers or sisters.

Social
- Will begin to play with others (**co-operative play**).
- Will play alone for long periods without adult attention.
- Will share and take turns.
- Can feed themselves skilfully.
- Can dress and undress.
- Can wash and dry hands and face, and clean teeth.

Toys and play

As for 3 years, plus counting and alphabet games, making collages, junk modelling, messy and creative play, simple board games, card games, e.g. snap, dressing-up and imaginative play. Outdoor toys could include skipping ropes, footballs, obstacle courses, toy gardening tools.

FIVE YEARS

By this age most children's physical skills are well developed and they are becoming more agile and skilful. Language and communications skills are also well developed. They enjoy imaginary games and team games, understanding the need for rules, and can co-operate with others.

Physical
Gross motor skills
- Can skip with a rope.
- Very skilful at climbing, sliding, swinging, jumping, etc.
- Can use a wide variety of large equipment confidently.
- Can throw a ball to a partner, catch and hit a ball with a bat with some accuracy.
- Can balance on one foot for several seconds.
- Can hop.
- Can dance rhythmically to music.

Fine motor skills
- Dresses and undresses with little help.
- Can complete more complex jigsaws with interlocking pieces.
- Can cut out shapes using scissors, more accurately.
- Can use a knife and fork when eating.
- Has good pencil control.
- Can colour in pictures neatly.

Sensory
- Matches 10–12 colours.
- Vision and hearing developing to adult level.

Intellectual – concepts
- Can distinguish between fact and fiction.
- Begins to understand the concept of measurement.
- Can count up to 20 by rote.
- Uses reasoning based on experience.
- Can understand right and wrong.
- Can understand simple rules and the need for them.
- Talks about past, present and future.
- May begin to read.
- Recognises name when written and tries to write it.
- Can copy, squares, triangles and letters V, T, H, O, X, G, A, U and Y.
- May write own name and simple words.
- Can draw a house with windows, door, chimney and roof
- Pictures now have a background, e.g. sky.
- Draws a person and head with one or two features.
- Can copy a circle but might not join it up.

Intellectual – language
- Speech is grammatically correct and more fluent.
- Enjoys jokes and riddles.

Social
- May start to play more with own sex.
- Beginning to choose own friends.
- Will play happily with other children.

Emotional
- Helps and comforts other children who are unhappy or hurt.
- Will respond to reasoning.
- Can still be selfish.

Toys and play

As for 4 years, plus more complex painting and drawing activities and jigsaws. Games with rules, books with more characters and detailed stories and pictures. Outdoors will enjoy team games, large climbing frames, mini-trampolines, hopscotch, catch and chase.

Appendix

 RESEARCH AND PRESENTATION CHECKLISTS

Try to use checklist similar to those below when working on your coursework to make sure that you have a good range of different types of research and methods of presentation. Remember you don't have to use them all!

TYPES AND KINDS OF RESEARCH

Primary research	✓	Secondary research	✓
Survey		Textbooks	
Questionnaire		Newspapers/magazines	
Interview		Leaflets	
Inventory		Internet	
Comparative investigation		TV programmes	
Photographs		Videos	
Visits		Letters/e-mail	
Others		Others	

METHODS OF PRESENTATION AND ICT

Presentation	✓
Handwritten text	
Sketches	
Spidergrams	
Charts	
Tables	
Pie charts	
Pictograms	
Scanned illustrations	
Magazine/catalogue pictures	
Word processed text	
DTP	
Clip-art	
Digital images	

© Hodder & Stoughton 2004

2 Appendix

→ **COURSEWORK CHECKLIST**

The checklist below might be useful when working on your coursework to help you to make sure that you are including everything you need to do. Check it out with your teacher first.

Step/Stage	What is needed	✓										
1. Introduction	First name/date of birth/age at start of study											
	Physical description											
	Personality											
	Family, home and local environment											
	Stage of physical development											
	Stage of intellectual development – language development											
	Stage of intellectual development – concept development											
	Stage of emotional development											
	Stage of social development											
2. Broad area of research (BAR)	Chosen area stated and explained											
	Reasons for choice linked to child and introduction											
3. Background research	Secondary research											
	Primary research											
	Variety of methods of presentation											
	Analysis and evaluation of BAR											
4. Focused area of research (FAR)	Chosen area stated and explained											
	Reasons for choice linked to child and introduction											
	Secondary research											
	Primary research											
	Variety of methods of presentation											
	Analysis and evaluation of BAR											
	Predictions made for FAR investigations/activities											

© Hodder & Stoughton 2004

Step/Stage	What is needed				✓
5. Planning visits and FAR investigations	Simple action plan				
6. (a) Visits	1 Aims/planning	Expectations	Record of visit	Evaluation	
	2 Aims/planning	Expectations	Record of visit	Evaluation	
	3 Aims/planning	Expectations	Record of visit	Evaluation	
	4 Aims/planning	Expectations	Record of visit	Evaluation	
	5 Aims/planning	Expectations	Record of visit	Evaluation	
	6 Aims/planning	Expectations	Record of visit	Evaluation	
6. (b) FAR investigations/activities	1 Aims/planning	Expectations	Record of activity	Evaluation	
	2 Aims/planning	Expectations	Record of activity	Evaluation	
	3 Aims/planning	Expectations	Record of activity	Evaluation	
7. Final evaluation	Comparison of child at end of study with introduction				
	Evaluation of PIES				
	Comment on any change and progression in child's development				
	Evaluation of FAR and FAR investigations/activities				

In each of the above stages have you given . . . ?	Specialist terms			
	Quotes			
	Personal opinions			
8. Bibliography	List of all books and websites used			
	List of computer programs used			
9. Appendix	Any research materials, e.g. leaflets, copies of questionnaires, drawings by child, etc.			

© Hodder & Stoughton 2004

3 Appendix

➡ WRITING UP YOUR VISITS

When marking your study, your teacher will look at how well you gather, record and collate your work. If you organise and write up your visits with clear headings, you will gain better marks.

Look at the following two ideas.
(If you are not doing a FAR activity miss out sections in red.)

IDEA 1

VISIT

Date
Age: **Years**   **Months**
Place
Length of visit
Aims of planning

Expectations

FAR aims and planning

FAR expectations

© Hodder & Stoughton 2004

Observations

Evaluations:
Physical

Intellectual

Emotional

Social

FAR activity/investigation and evaluation

© Hodder & Stoughton 2004

IDEA 2

VISIT

Date
Age of child   (Give the same information for each visit.)
Place
Length of visit

Aims
(State the areas of development you are looking at and describe the activity/activities planned.)

Planning and organisation
(Briefly describe planning, safety, paints, materials needed, etc.)

Predictions
(What you expect the child to do – link to theory.)

Observation
(Written details of visit.)

© Hodder & Stoughton 2004

Evaluation
   (Write up evaluation of PIES; try to link with aims and predictions.)

FAR activity/investigation – aims and planning
   (Briefly describe what you have chosen to do and how you will do it.)

FAR expectations
   (What do you expect to find out? Try to link this with your research.)

Record of FAR

Evaluation
   (Write up your conclusion – try to link to your expectations and research.)

© Hodder & Stoughton 2004

4 Appendix

SOME USEFUL WEBSITES

www.bbc.co.uk www.bbc.co.uk/parenting/childcare www.bbc.cbeebies/grownups	A huge range of articles and information on all aspects of child development and caring for children, including having a baby, learning, ideas for activities to help learning and development.
www.babycentre.co.uk	Wide range of articles and information on all aspects of pregnancy. Birth, care of babies and toddlers. Some good information on developmental milestones.
www.babyworld.co.uk	General information on aspects of child care and development. Interesting section on testing and evaluation of toys and other equipment.
www.family/fun.go.uk	American website with some ideas on activities for children.
www.nurseryworld.co.uk	Some good ideas on activities for young children to help various areas of development, e.g. creative and physical development, communication and language.
www.btha.co.uk	British toy and hobbies association with information on toy safety and regulations.
www.elc.co.uk	Early learning centre website with information and ideas on toys, puzzles, games and activities for different types of development.
www.fisher-price.com	Information on toys by age and type, and learning through play.
www.tomy.co.uk	Information on toys for different ages.

© Hodder & Stoughton 2004

www.rospa.co.uk	Information on road, home, water, play, product safety, etc.
www.capt.org.uk	Child accident prevention trust website. Information on all aspects of child safety.
www.boots.com	Some useful information on babies, children and health issues.
www.batr.co.uk	Website for British Association of Toy Retailers with a lot of information on toys, toy safety and history of toys.
www.toysafety.net	Some information on potentially dangerous toys.
www.bupa.co.uk	Useful information on childcare options including childminders, nannies, nurseries, etc. Detailed ABC of health covering lots of child related topics, e.g. weaning, babysitting, learning, children at home.
www.lmu.ac.uk/stuserv/childcare/ choosing/htm	Information on choosing different childcare options.
www.qca.org.uk	Information on the Foundation Curriculum and Early Learning Goals.
www.pampers.com	Information on all aspects of childcare, including developmental milestones. Good ideas for toys and activities for all ages.
www.nutrition.org.uk	Useful information on healthy eating under BNF Schools and Education Parent Area.
www.nctpregnancyandbabycare.com	Information on pregnancy, birth and care up to 12 months.
www.under5s.co.uk	Search engine for information on a wide range of topics about the under 5s.

© Hodder & Stoughton 2004

Appendix

➡ EXAMPLE OF A PLANNING SHEET FOR VISITS

Visit	Date	Activity/Activities	Planning needs	P	I	E	S
1	Sept 27	Baking cookies and decorating					
2	Oct 29						
3	Nov 12						
4	Dec 14						
FAR	Dec 14	Inventory of indoor toys					
5	Jan 10						
FAR	Jan 10	Inventory of outdoor toys					
6	Feb 15						
FAR	Feb 15	Interview with parents					

Key: FAR = focused area of research.

© Hodder & Stoughton 2004

Appendix

 RISK ASSESSMENT

Visit No Date Place					
Brief description of activity					
		Danger level			
What is the possible danger	**Why is it dangerous**	**High**	**Medium**	**Low**	**How can it be prevented (control measure)**

© Hodder & Stoughton 2004

Appendix

➡ EVALUATING YOUR OBSERVATIONS

Physical Development	Intellectual Development
Social Development	Emotional Development

© Hodder & Stoughton 2004

Appendix

➡ SOME USEFUL WORDS AND PHRASES

Physical		Intellectual	Emotional	Social
Gross Motor	**Fine Motor**			
balancing	ambidextrous	acquire	anxiety	aggressive
bear-walking	building	babbling	attention	attachment
bending	clutching	communicating	bonding	attention
bouncing	cutting out	concentrating	boredom	seeking
catching	dressing	concepts	comforter	attitudes
clapping	fastening	copying	confidence	behaviour
climbing	zipper/button	creative	control	bladder control
co-ordination	fine muscular	curious	defiant	caring
crawling	control	echolalia	dummy	cleaning teeth
cruising	grasping	egocentric	excitable	considerate
dancing	hand–eye co-	encourage	excitement	co-operative
hopping	ordination	experience	fear	play
jumping	inferior pincer	exploring	feelings	cultural
kicking	grasp	genes	frustration	curious
lifting	interlocking	imagining	happiness	friendly
muscular	joining	imitating	jealous	independence
pedalling	left-handed	independent	love	joining in
running	making	investigating	moody	manners
shuffling	mature pincer	jargon	nail biting	parallel (play)
sitting	grasp	knowledge	negative	please
skipping	modelling	language	emotion	polite
sliding	palmar grasp	learning	nightmare	regression
squatting	passing	listening	positive	separation
standing	picking up	looking	emotion	anxiety
stirring	pincer grasp	nature and	praise	share
swimming	placing	nurture	sadness	shy
swinging	pointing	object	scared	social skill
throwing	posting	permanence	scream	solitary (play)
twisting	primitive tripod	perception	self-confidence	stranger
walking	grasp	questions	self-image	take turns
	reflex	remember	self-esteem	thank you
	right-handed	stimulate	separation	toilet training
	sticking	talking	anxiety	washing hands
	stringing	telegraphic	shriek	
	threading	sentences	stress	
	tripod grasp	understand	temper	
	turning (pages)		tantrums	
			temperament	
			thumb sucking	
			worry	

© Hodder & Stoughton 2004

Appendix

➡ WORDS THAT CONNECT OR START SENTENCES

In writing up your coursework the following words might be useful. They either *connect* or *start* sentences.

First(ly). . . .	Also. . . .	In particular. . . .
Second(ly). . . .	Moreover. . . .	Above all. . . .
Then. . . .	As a result. . . .	Notably. . . .
. . . .and then. . . .	Equally. . . .	Specifically. . . .
. . . .after(wards)	Similarly. . . .	. . . .especially. . . .
Meanwhile. . . .	Likewise. . . .	
During. . . .	In the same way. . . .	For example. . . .
Whenever. . . .	As with. . . .	. . . . such as. . . .
Eventually. . . .		
Finally. . . .		Clearly. . . .
	However. . . .	. . . . of course. . . .
In addition. . . .	. . . . but. . . .	. . . . the following. . . .
Furthermore. . . .	Nevertheless. . . .	
Therefore. . . .	Alternatively. . . .	In brief. . . .
Consequently. . . .	Despite this. . . .	On the whole. . . .
. . . .because/as. . . .	. . . .instead. . . .	To sum up. . . .
accordingly. . . .	Whereas. . . .	
. . . .as long as. . . .	Although	In conclusion. . . .

➡ TERMS USED IN COURSEWORK INCLUDE:

Analyse: Break down issues/ideas into parts and examine how the parts are related.

Assess: Make informed judgement about how good/effective something is based on an awareness of strengths and weaknesses; present a reasoned analysis.

Evaluate: Give a judgement or opinion as to the worth of something; judgements should be reasoned and whenever possible be supported by arguments or facts from books, articles, etc.

Outline: Offer a summary, e.g. a brief description of planned research/methods.

© Hodder & Stoughton 2004